HOMEOWNER'S GUIDE TO
LANDSCAPE DESIGN

HOMEOWNER'S GUIDE TO
LANDSCAPE DESIGN

SECOND EDITION

Timothy M. Michel

Illustrated by the Author

The Countryman Press

WOODSTOCK, VERMONT

The illustrations on pages 20, 30, 35, 103, 106,
are by Albert Azzarone

Cover design by Wladislaw Finne
Text design by David Robinson

Library of Congress Cataloging in Publication Data

Michel, Timothy M.
  Homeowner's guide to landscape design.

  Bibliography: p. 162
  Includes index.
  1. Landscape architecture.   2. Landscape gardening.
I. Title.
SB473.M46   1983   712'.6   82-22047
ISBN 0-914378-94-5

Printed in the United States of America
by Whitman Press, Lebanon, New Hampshire

TO MY FATHER

CONTENTS

vii

ACKNOWLEDGEMENTS

It is hard to single out a few people from the many who could be easily acknowledged here, but among them would have to be: Virginia Pender, Michael Vergason, Harry Porter, Gary Okerlund, Peter and Jane Jennison, and Chris Lloyd for their advice and support.

Introduction

WHY LANDSCAPE YOUR HOME?

The primary reason for landscaping is to match more efficiently and pleasantly the inherent characteristics of your land with your needs. Thoughtful landscaping offers you more attractive and usable surroundings while dramatically increasing the resale value of your home. It makes your house and property complementary to one another by marrying the indoor and outdoor spaces and activities.

Landscaping can provide privacy, screen unpleasant views, buffer winds, prevent erosion, increase energy efficiency, provide shade, organize circulation patterns, and solve a myriad of other home problems. What to do about poorly drained areas? How to screen your neighbor's new home? Where to put the driveway turn-around? These and dozens of similar problems can be solved in a comprehensive landscape plan. Conversely, the positive aspects of your land can be enhanced with such a plan: a view exposed, a stand of trees accented, a southern exposure taken advantage of, and other, often unexpected, values revealed.

There is a common misconception that landscaping is an expensive, decorative frill. Actually, it can be an eminently practical, functional and relatively inexpensive part of your total home environment. I am not speaking here of a few plants thrown in as an afterthought, but of the full and efficient use of your land. With scarcities cropping up everywhere, it is a fortunate person who has even a small plot of ground to call his own. And the smaller the property, the more important careful landscape planning and design become. Where space is at a premium every square foot

1

of the land must be made to count if you are to get the maximum benefit from your property.

Energy conservation is another often-neglected reason to landscape. We can no longer afford to waste space or ignore the critical factors of climate and site characteristics on our energy consumption. Properly siting a new home for maximum solar exposure and using plant materials for windscreens, shade, and insulation around a new or existing one has a surprisingly significant effect on lowering fuel consumption. Plants and other architectural landscape elements like fences can direct air flow, channeling cool, summer breezes and blocking chilling winter winds. Deciduous trees planted on the dwelling's southern exposure provide needed summer shade and then drop their leaves to allow maximum winter sun. Evergreen shrubs near walls create "dead air" space which acts as excellent insulation, preventing rapid heat loss through the walls. Hedges can be planted as windbreaks to temper the climate, making your yard warmer in the winter and cooler in summer. In winter a windbreak not only serves to cut off chilling winds, but also acts as a snow fence to keep blowing snow out of walks and driveways.

In the same way that a protected shrub may grow far north of its natural habitat, an energy-conscious landscape plan can modify the climate around the home and lower your fuel needs. It is possible for a wind-protected dwelling, whose landscape has been planned for both beauty and energy conservation, to cut fuel consumption by as much as twenty-five percent! Even an existing home can cut energy costs by fifteen percent and fifteen percent of your annual heating bill quickly adds up to a substantial savings.

Landscaping pays in other ways too. Real estate values are enhanced by good landscape planning and design. Done well, it adds to a property's permanent value and makes resale easier. The incorporation of a deck or patio into a dwelling is only the most obvious example of this. Actually, all properly planned landscape "improvements" can be viewed as sound investments. This is especially true in today's escalating housing market where the demand for efficiency, space utilization, and outdoor access are rapidly increasing.

An attractive landscape is always a positive selling point in any home. It is estimated that a pleasant lawn with well placed trees and shrubs adds at least ten percent to the price of a home.

Terraces, patios, fencing, trellises and other highly visible improvements can boost that to fifteen to twenty percent. Improvements like these add usable living space to a property by creating "outdoor rooms."

Real estate resale values vary considerably depending on a property's location. In general, though, as long as the improvements are not overly luxurious or high-maintenance items, homeowners will more than recoup their initial expenses. With the median price of a house topping $70,000, it is plain common sense to make the most of your property—both for your present enjoyment and for its eventual increased resale value. After all, your home is probably the biggest single investment you will ever make.

In our mobile society, even the transient household can still do a great deal with its landscape in a short time. Knowing that you may only be in a home for a year or two is no reason not to improve your surroundings. Often a few simple changes will make your temporary home a much more enjoyable place while you are in residence and will reap you economic reward when you move on.

A well conceived landscape completes a home by tying it to the land. It makes the house a part of the landscape and vice versa and provides transition areas between them. The property can become a unified "place", rather than just a plot with a house on it. Even the most ordinary tract home can be given some degree of character and uniqueness this way.

Perhaps the most compelling reason for landscaping your property is the special opportunity it offers you to shape your own personal environment—the home landscape. Your property is a private retreat in our increasingly hectic and homogenized world. The chance to plan and design these everyday surroundings to fit your individual needs offers both a closer relationship with nature and the rare opportunity to create a more positive environment within which to live. Do not let this slip away. You do not have to be either wealthy or a "green thumb" to enjoy the benefits of a landscaped home.

The question becomes no longer why landscape, but how. The answer: according to a plan. A well developed landscape plan insures a rational design for your *entire* property, instead of a hodge-podge of piecemeal, weekend projects that have little

HOW TO GO ABOUT IT

relationship to one another. Planning organizes all these pieces into a harmonious whole and enables you to maximize your property's potential.

It also avoids mistakes. How many times have you heard the lament, "Now that it's done, I wish we'd done it differently." The terrace should have been brick, the garden should have been here, and so on. Doing it right the first time is the essence of planning. It almost guarantees better results.

This is not to say that a beautiful landscape cannot exist without a plan. Many older properties were developed without one, but many years of experimentation have gone into their haphazard creation. Planning can shorten this trial and error period to weeks or even days.

Another reason for developing an overall landscape plan is that it allows you to "phase" different parts of your design over a period of years. You decide which things to do and when—staging the plan's implementation to fit your priorities, time schedule and budget. Since there is a plan being followed, each phase will still be a part of your property's orderly development. Moreover, a finished landscape plan is detailed and specific enough for fairly accurate cost estimates to be made from it, making budgeting much simpler. Following an overall plan, then, lets you take on single, manageable projects one at a time and still end up with a unified, practical and aesthetically pleasing *complete* design.

CHAPTER 1

How to Use This Book

This book is for the resourceful property owner—a do-it-yourself guide for the initial development or improvement of the home landscape. The landscape design process and accompanying guidelines outlined here are equally applicable to urban, suburban and rural situations, regardless of scale, region or lifestyle. The reason for this flexibility is simple. The process is designed to synthesize what you have—the existing landscape—with what you need. The step-by-step priority decisions you make as you proceed will provide the framework within which you can sensibly design your own surroundings.

The same steps apply whether you are starting to build on an undeveloped piece of land, landscaping a lot with a new home, or relandscaping an already developed property. As the "planner-designer" you are the crucial factor. By following the process through each step you will be able to:

1. Evaluate your own immediate living environment.
2. Identify and clarify your priorities for its development.
3. Test and formalize these priorities into a landscape design.

First, in examining your site, its individual opportunities and constraints will begin to appear. By formulating a program for its use—the "what do I want" stage—you establish your own priorities. Once you have an understanding of the land and have established these priorities, both to capture your site's positive features and to avoid or minimize the negative ones, you have an established framework for designing. The land's characteristics and your priorities are like the pieces of the puzzle. The site conditions and your needs dictate the shape of these pieces. The art of putting them together is design.

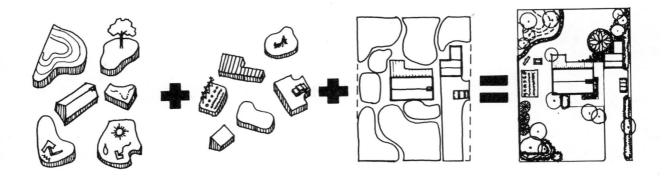

This process is valid at any level of landscape design. First consider the land: soil conditions, local weather problems, shade, and other existing conditions; then your priorities: is the backyard a place to entertain or retreat, and how do you want to develop it? After this comes the designing. The type of treatment called for will become more obvious once you have determined these other factors.

THE PROCESS

The seven steps to the design process are:

1. Reading the Land: The Search for Design Clues. The purpose of this initial step is twofold. First, it encourages you to take a fresh look at your property—free of preconceived ideas. It then helps you discover the inherent characteristics of the land which can serve as clues to its development.

2. Preparing the Base Map. A base map serves as the backdrop for your future drawings. It provides a two-dimensional representation of your property from which you can begin to plan and design.

3. Identifying Existing Conditions. What do you have to work with? The property's characteristics and its inherent assets and constraints—its good and bad points—must be identified and mapped.

4. Deciding What You Want. Step 4 establishes your program for the site. What do you and your family want and need in your outdoor space? This involves first listening to everyone's desires and then assigning them priority values. So you end up knowing not only what everyone involved wants, but how important each item is in relation to the others. Put another way, desires divided by priorities equal needs.

$$\frac{\text{desires}}{\text{priorities}} = \text{needs}$$

5. Diagramming Activity Areas. Using the base map as a guide, you can now assign appropriate locations and approximate size requirements to each of your established needs, such as a terrace, a barbecue, or an herb garden.

6. Designing the Overall Scheme. The diagrammed activity areas are here taken a step further and translated into a rough design. This is the intermediate design stage and the placement and interrelationship between the activity areas should be checked and refined. Are they compatible? Are they well connected and easily accessible? Don't hesitate to try several different arrangements on the base map before one is decided upon.

7. Finishing the Design. This final step takes the chosen overall design scheme to completion. It is concerned with the detail level of design. For example, not where should the walkway or terrace go, but rather which material is most suitable and what are the proper dimensions for it. Once this information is formalized on paper you have a finished design from which the project can be constructed. You are ready to build.

By following this design process, you will be approaching your landscape logically, beginning with the planning steps and only then moving on to the design elements. After all, how can you begin to design, unless you first have an understanding of the land and have decided what you want in your landscape? All too often today this vital planning stage is overlooked in a premature concern for plants and plant species.

This is partly because relatively little has been written that focuses on how to plan and design residential landscapes. These terms still intimidate people, either because they do not know where to begin or because they have not been convinced it is necessary. Whether you are an intensive gardener or a homeowner who has only belatedly recognized the value of your landscape, this guide is intended to fill that gap. It is not a plant book. It is a landscape planning and design manual, intended to help you create a functional and aesthetically pleasing outdoor environment for you and your family. With it you will be able to avoid numerous pitfalls, while producing an organized landscape plan responsive to both the land and your needs.

Designing your own landscape is *not* beyond your capabilities and can be a richly rewarding experience. If you are willing to give the project the time and energy it deserves, you can do a great deal. If you have the option of hiring a professional landscape architect, by all means do so; but if not, you should feel capable of going ahead on your own.

I can almost hear some of you bemoaning your lack of creative talent. Stop! Everyone can be creative and designing is not the exclusive domain of artists. Your "pieces"—the site itself and your priorities for it—will of themselves point towards solutions. They offer strong hints as to what to do. Listen to them. The logical step-by-step process will reveal proper design solutions for you to pursue. The key is organizing the property so that your needs fit compatibly into the site's conditions.

Everyone is a part-time designer. Numerous everyday activities incorporate design. Packing a suitcase or shopping bag, deciding what to wear, cooking a meal . . . all these activities call on you to plan, order, arrange and coordinate different elements in a coherent, pleasing and efficient manner, i.e., to design them.

Keep in mind that there is never only one "correct" solution. Within the constraints of the process you have followed there may be several. Ultimately, the best one is a matter of preference on your part, but remember that "good" design is usually simple and straightforward.

Any landscape problem, no matter how small, is part of a larger environment. It is always important to remember the property's larger context if the proposed changes are to "fit" and become an integral part of your overall landscape plan. The more aspects you consider in your planning stage, the greater the likelihood the design will prove to be a successful one.

Obviously, the degree to which you pursue each of the individual steps depends upon the kind and magnitude of your problem. Siting a new home, for example, requires extensive site analysis, while planning a deck does not. However, it is essential that any landscape problem be approached in the two stages: *planning* and then *designing.*

This approach should also be kept in mind when house-hunting or buying "raw" land, especially in choosing among various properties. In these cases, site analysis and the initial process steps are crucial. Ask yourself: do the landscape characteristics of the existing home or the undeveloped parcel correspond to your proposed uses? Matching your needs with the different sites can quickly determine your best choice.

Carrying out these early process steps assures the proper organization of your outdoor space. If you are building on an undeveloped site, they can directly influence the design, location, and even the interior layout of the new home itself. With a new house on an unlandscaped lot, these planning steps not only create functional outdoor arrangements but may also suggest minor alterations in the house to better connect the building with the landscape. And in an older home they help to bring out and improve the special characteristics which already exist. In using the design process in these three situations the only difference is in the number of pre-existing conditions to work with and the corresponding limitations on the designer's flexibility. The process remains valid in each case.

Once beyond the planning stage, Steps 1 to 5, you are ready to design. Chapter 7 includes a review of the major principles and elements of site design to help you translate the information you have gathered into an overall design scheme. Other general design guidelines and helpful hints have also been added to make your job easier. Again, between Steps 6 and 7 additional chapters have been included; this time to ease the transition from the overall design scheme (Chapter 9) to your finished landscape plan. The first of these, Chapter 10, focuses on the materials and do's and don'ts of the various landscape areas such as driveways, terraces, walls and entryways. Chapter 11 deals with planting design and the selection of plant materials.

With Step 7 your landscape plan will be finished and Part I of the book completed. The second part, "Construction and Maintenance," will help make your plan become a reality. It covers site preparation, job supervision and staging and is also concerned with the proper management of your home landscape for long life and beauty.

All of this can seem a little overwhelming at first. The whole design process may appear too time-consuming and detailed for you. Don't despair. Actually, you will find that the process moves along fairly quickly once you begin.

I have purposely tried to cover every contingency as thoroughly as possible. Remember that much of the information may not be pertinent in your particular situation. What is most important is that you understand and follow the correct sequence in approaching your landscape problems: planning, designing, construction and maintenance.

PART I

PLANNING AND DESIGNING YOUR LANDSCAPE

CHAPTER 2

Step 1/Reading the Land:
The Search for Design Clues

A landscape architect friend of mine once commented that his designs "grew out of the ground." What he meant was that the land inspired him and showed him what and how to design. He was able to heed the design clues inherent in the landscape itself. Understanding your landscape and knowing how to develop it are one and the same thing, so "reading" the land is a very important first step.

To do this correctly, it is often necessary to take a fresh look at your property. Too often homeowners approach their properties with eyes blinded by preconceived ideas. They are determined to have this or that, right down to specific plant species, regardless of whether it fits their needs, the land, or the architectural style of the house.

One easy way to begin with a clean slate is to get up and take a slow walk around your property and just look. This first step is just as valid for relandscaping an older home as it is for developing a new site. Try to attune yourself to your surroundings. It's a good idea to take a note pad along with you to jot down what you see. If you are a photographer you might want to bring your camera. A compass will prove handy too.

While you are walking notice your property's orientation to the sun, the types of vegetation growing, the views, slopes, the proximity to neighboring buildings, and any special features of the land such as a spring, a major tree, or rock outcroppings. What does it feel like—a meadow, a forest, a courtyard, a neglected garden? Sometimes it helps to compile a list of the good and

bad aspects of your site as you go around it. Is it private? Easy to maintain? Observe the "lay of the land." Are drainage problems apparent? Rock outcroppings may mean it will be too costly to include a basement in a new home. Is the soil sandy or clay-like? That will influence your choice of plant material. Make notes on all your observations no matter how trivial they may seem. Later, these notes, especially the key words, will tell you a great deal. The photographs will be useful too. You can re-familiarize yourself with the landscape at a glance—even design from them.

To many people this will sound like a waste of time. You already know what your property is like. The truth is, you probably don't and may have never looked at your land with the intent of understanding it. Let the site speak for itself. Clues to its eventual design or re-design will begin to evolve and surface, if you have an open mind.

Be sure to look beyond your property line too. Nature knows no man-made boundaries, and clues to your landscape may be apparent from your property's surroundings. In a very real sense your landscape includes everything you can see from the site and everything that affects it. A distant hillside or a neighbor's fine, old tree should not be ignored just because they are not on your land. In the same way, run-off onto your property from higher ground, noise from a public highway, or an unpleasant view must be considered in your designing. To know your property you must understand it in the context of its surroundings. Not only should all the elements within a design relate to one another, but the design as a whole must "fit" into its surroundings.

In any case, it is never a waste of time to walk around your house or property. Trying to clear your mind of all your preconceived ideas—to take a fresh look—is both useful and enjoyable. For your own sake, don't go out and think: "that's where I am putting the deck and such and such a plant goes here!" Just look. Everything you learn from this little outing will prove helpful to you later. The inspirations that make landscape design an art come from nature itself, so pay attention.

File your notes and photographs away for now, but we'll be pulling them out later when we begin designing.

CHAPTER 3

Step 2/Preparing Your Base Map

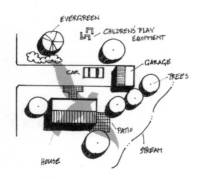

A base map is like a bird's eye view of your property from directly overhead.

A base map or plot plan is a two-dimensional, symbolic representation of a three-dimensional space showing all of the existing features on a piece of property. It shows the details as they would appear from directly above your site. A finished base map shows the property boundaries, the location of any structures, orientation to the sun, all important trees and shrubs, and any other natural and man-made features of the site. It must be drawn as closely as possible to scale to locate everything properly.

Once completed, this map will serve as the basis for all your design work. It is invaluable in avoiding later mistakes and oversights. A plot plan helps you to visualize and test your designs for spatial requirements, interrelationships between activity areas and composition. Remember, a mistake on the ground is not easy to correct, but a design error in your plan is easily erased.

If you happen to have a property deed, a contour map, or a house plan, your work is partially done for you already. A deed survey will show the dimensions of your property in feet. This can be expanded into a full-blown base map. Contour plans are less common, but extremely useful, especially if your property has considerable grade changes. Grade in this context refers to changes in the degree of slope, i.e., how much the land rises or falls over a given distance. A property map that shows contours adds the third dimension to your base map. Reading contour maps takes practice. The accompanying sketches will help. If your land is unusually hilly or very flat you may want to consider

16

going to the expense of having a topographic survey done. Any land surveyor is equipped to do this and can provide you with a finished base map in the process.

A house plan is useful once you have located the home itself within your property. It shows the location of all the doors and windows—information you will need in relating interior and exterior spaces.

If you are lucky enough to have any of these maps, make a note of their scales and be prepared to transfer all the information onto your new base plan.

If your home has not yet been located or designed, using your prepared base map as a guide and proceeding through Steps 2 and 3 of the design process, you will be in an excellent position to site it properly within the property and arrange its interior layout to best advantage.

With or without existing plans it is relatively simple to construct a base map. The easiest way is the "grid method." All you need is:

—50 or 100 foot measuring tape (and someone to hold the other end).

—a 17″ by 22″ or larger sheet of graph paper with 10 squares to the inch. Graph paper sheets are available at most stationery or art supply stores. (This will cover a lot 170′ x 220′. Larger sizes are available if needed.)

—a roll or several sheets of large tracing paper and several thick pencils, or felt tip pens.

—a large ball of string, stakes, or flagged nails.

Using the tape, measure and record all the dimensions of the house, locate major trees, property lines, driveways, walks, and other stationary features. This will take several hours, but is time well spent. This map is the foundation of your plan.

In order to locate objects within a grid it is best to work from several, fixed points. Foundation lines, house corners, and property lines will serve as excellent fixed points. Located first, these points will act as a reference for your later measurements.

Imaginary base lines can then be established between the fixed points and your grid will begin to take shape. With a base line established, you can determine the locations of objects near

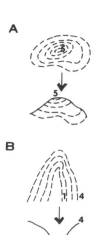

A small knoll (A) and a ditch (B) as they would appear *in plan* and in *elevation.*

MAKING YOUR OWN MAP

Scales: using the graph paper described, the drawing scale is 1′ = 10′ (i.e. one inch on the graph equals ten feet).

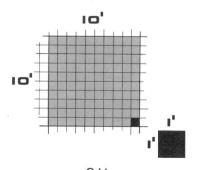

Grid

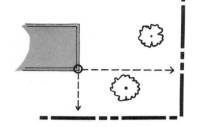

Begin your measurements from fixed (immobile) points. In this case the corner of an existing home is being used to locate the boundary fences.

that line fairly accurately. Temporarily marking these imaginary base lines with string, stakes, or flagged nails will help the job go faster and increase accuracy. Be sure to locate the object at a 90° angle from the base line.

Once you have these measurements transfer them onto your graph paper. This is done by treating each square or grid as equal to one foot. Since there are ten small squares to an inch, a scale of one inch = ten feet is established. Using a 17 by 22 inch graph paper sheet this scale allows you to map an area of 170 by 220 feet. If your particular site is larger, either tape two or more 17 by 22 inch sheets together, buy a larger sheet, or treat each of

By measuring out from the fixed point with a tape measure to the property boundaries additional fixed points and base lines between them have been set up here. (On the ground, it may help to temporarily mark base lines with string for later reference.)

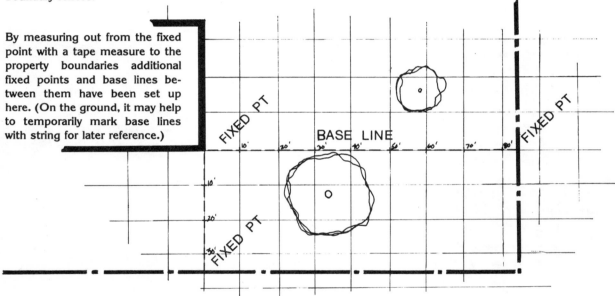

Locating an object off the base line is done by lining up the object at a right angle (90°) from the measured base line. The distance in feet out from the fixed point will be known. Now you have only to determine the number of feet off the base line the object lies. For reasonable accuracy the measuring tape *must* be pulled at a right angle from the base line. This can be done roughly by eye, but it may be helpful to use something square such as a window screen or carpenter's square to check your eye line.

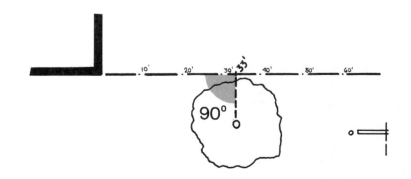

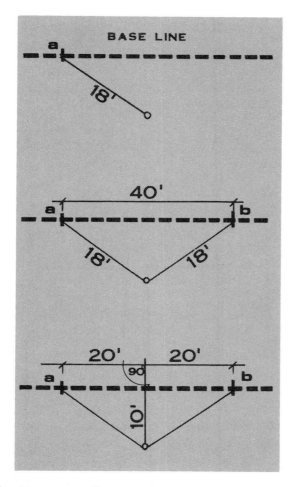

To insure a 90° angle where a high degree of accuracy is necessary try the following: At a point (a) along the base line pull the tape to the object at a roughly 45° angle. Measure the distance. In the example shown the distance is eighteen feet. Measure the same distance back to the base line in the opposite direction (b). Now measure the distance along the base line between points a and b. The midpoint between them will always be at 90° from the object.

the small grids as equalling two feet, thereby creating a scale of one inch = twenty feet. It may not always be necessary to include your whole property on your base map. With several acres or more or where only a portion of the property is going to be worked on, it is possible to restrict your base map to that immediate area.

Using a tape measure to accurately locate your primary fixed points and all other major features near the house is important. However, your "exact" measurements to all objects can be somewhat flexible. This is not meant to encourage you to use rough measurements! Any measurements of secondary features taken roughly will have to be treated as such in your plan. How-

SHORTCUTS FOR ROUGH MEASUREMENTS

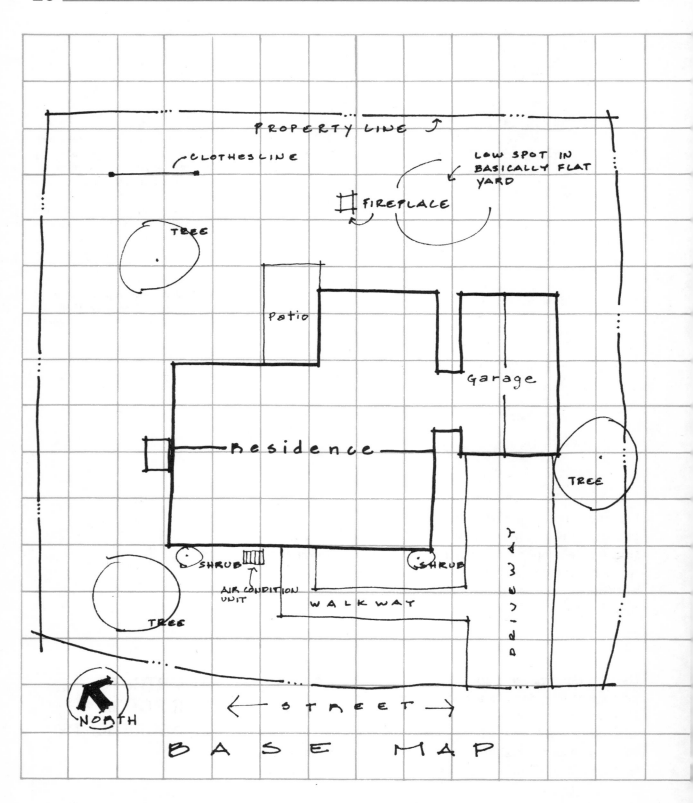

PROPERTY LINE ↗

CLOTHESLINE

LOW SPOT IN
BASICALLY FLAT
YARD

FIREPLACE

TREE

Patio

Garage

Residence

TREE

SHRUB

SHRUB

AIR CONDITION
UNIT

WALKWAY

DRIVEWAY

TREE

NORTH

← STREET →

B A S E   M A P

ever, accepting that the temptation to cut corners is strong, here are two easy ways to *roughly* determine distance and elevation (grade).

Pacing off a distance is fairly accurate. First measure your normal stride. Since a round number is simpler to work with, practice making your pace average three feet. It is then easy to determine any distance by multiplying the number of paces by three feet. If you begin to pace off a distance from a fixed point, you will be able to locate an object fairly well on your plan. As with the tape, pacing to an object from two known locations will increase the accuracy.

On a hilly site it is possible to roughly determine grade changes over open distances by "eyeballing." To do this you yourself act as a vertical measuring rod. The elevations are set to your eye level. Approximate: if you are six feet tall, assume your eye-level to be six feet. Beginning at the top of a rise gradually walk down and away, checking often, until your eyes are level with the top. Mark the spot you are standing on and repeat the procedure as far as needed. If the paces are counted between each eye-level mark you can approximate not only the grade change, or vertical drop, but the slope as well.

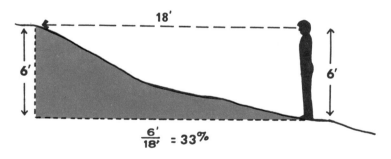

Another alternative involves two people and an 8 to 10 foot pole. The pole is measured off at 6 inch intervals. One person acts as the eyeballer, the other proceeds away from him with the measuring rod to the spot where elevation readings are required. Whatever the point on the pole is level with the reader's eye-level is then the vertical change in height—within six inches. This increases accuracy considerably and a measuring pole or rod is easy to construct. A long pole marked with tape will do admirably.

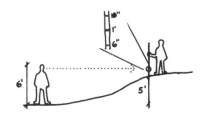

No matter what method you use, all the distances and locations should be transferred to your base map. Now, using the compass, add a north arrow to establish the property's orientation to the sun and the base map is completed.

NOTE: If you have existing maps of your property or residence they were probably drawn in architects' scales of ½″ = 1′ or ⅛″ = 1′. For convenience you should translate these professional drawings onto your graph paper using the one inch equals one foot scale. Or you may choose to use these drawings as your base map. If you do, be sure to draw everything in the appropriate scale and get an architects' ruler with the correct scale on it.

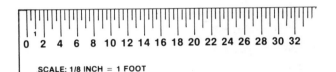

SCALE: 1/8 INCH = 1 FOOT

CHAPTER 4

Step 3/Identifying Existing Conditions: What Do You Have to Work With?

With a piece of tracing paper placed over your base map or on a Xeroxed copy of it, you should now graphically depict all the existing conditions of your property. What have you got to work with? Any notes or pictures you took in Step 1 may come in handy now. Many natural and man-made forces are being exerted on your land and many of them will affect your development of it. All the possible factors must at least be considered and any that apply directly to your home landscape belong on your existing conditions map.

SUN ORIENTATION

First note the orientation to the sun. The sun's path and intensity in your region of the country will determine the type and best location of your outdoor spaces as well as the kinds of plants that can grow there. Remember that the sun's "arc" changes with the seasons—high in summer and nearer to the horizon in winter. Direct winter sun is usually desirable, with some shade provided for the hotter months. A well oriented home, shaded in the summer by deciduous trees but open to winter sunlight when these leaves fall, is more energy efficient and can cut your heating and air-conditioning bills considerably.

Put an arc onto your plan showing the sun's "average" path across your property. The average path corresponds to the beginning of spring and fall. If the sun's differing heights are particularly important in your planning, show three arcs depicting

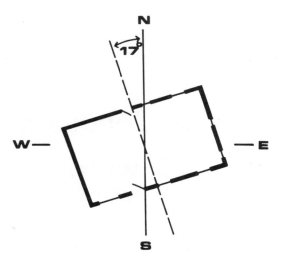

Ideal orientation of a home towards the sun. Note that most of windows are on the south and east side, while the west wall is solid against winter winds.

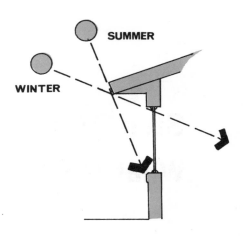

Angles of the sun in winter and summer at 43° Latitude North. This roof overhang blocks hot summer sun, but allows warming winter sun in. The 43° Latitude runs roughly between New York City and the California—Oregon border.

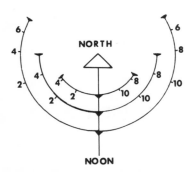

SUN AZIMUTH. By lining up the North arrow in this diagram with North on your base map you will have an idea of the arcs the sun forms over your property. The outer arc represents summer, the middle one fall, and the inner one winter. The numbers stand for clock hours. This azimuth is for 38° Latitude North—roughly across the middle of the United States from Washington, D.C., through St. Louis to San Francisco.

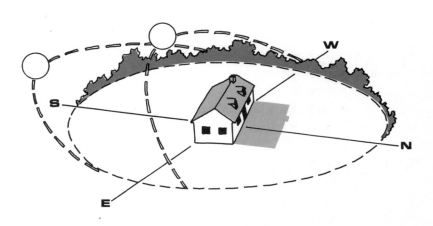

Winter and summer sun arcs over a property

the high, low and average sun heights: winter, summer, spring and fall. (See sun azimuth diagram.)

WIND

Next put arrows coming into the site showing the general wind directions. There are usually two major wind directions—winter winds and summer breezes. If you are unsure of the prevailing, local wind directions, check with the area weather bureau, TV stations, think back to windy days and ask your neighbors. Capable of cooling you on a warm day or chilling you on a cold one, winds are an important design factor. With preplanning, their direction and intensity can be modified to suit your site.

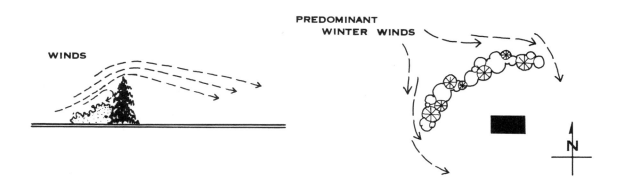

WINDS

PREDOMINANT WINTER WINDS

N

Windbreaks can deflect winds from two to five times their height, i.e., a ten foot hedge can control wind flow and velocity for a distance between twenty and fifty feet depending on the areodynamics of the windbreak itself. Windscreens can also be used to deflect undesirable winds away from or around your home.

VIEWS

Both good and bad views should be identified by arrows facing out from the site. For a view within your boundary show the arrow going to it; if the view is outside the property have the arrow pierce the property line. Be sure to note any pleasant or objectionable views from within the house as well as those only seen from outside. Also identify any potential views: for example, if those shrubs were cleared away would the exposed view be a desirable one?

ZONING RESTRICTIONS

Many properties are subject to various zoning restrictions such as set-back building lines. Check with local authorities for any restrictions that would affect your landscape planning. The more built-up your community, the likelier such restrictions exist. Some communities have adopted restrictions to cover everything from the height of fences to ordinances dealing with detached structures and swimming pools. Call local authorities with prepared questions and explain your situation. You can usually ask general questions without identifying yourself or the property in question. A copy of the local ordinances can also be useful, but be warned that they are frequently difficult to decipher without assistance.

UTILITIES

All utility connections should be shown on your base map: underground electrical and telephone wiring, sewage, gas and water lines, septic drain fields, and so forth. Also show any outside electrical and water outlets on your home itself. If any easements cross your property be sure to note those as well. Most of this information may appear on your deed map or house plan, but if there is any doubt as to the location of a utility connection, call their local representative. You will *definitely* need to know where utilities run before any extensive digging is done.

SOIL

The type and quality of your soil should be checked. It too is an existing condition. Is it sandy? Clay-like? Soil is a design factor that affects the plants you choose, the type of drainage (water absorption) you can expect, and the efficiency of any planned septic drainage fields. [One easy test for clay is to tightly hold a fist-full of your soil for a minute or so. If it does not fall apart when you release it, and shows your fingers indented, you probably have a high clay content.]

The pH level of your soil is also crucial to the type of plants it will support. The pH level records the degree of acidity or alkalinity in the soil. Several small and inexpensive soil-testing kits are now on the market and are usually available at hardware stores and nurseries. In most areas the local county Extension Service will test your soil free of charge and offer recommendations on how to improve it. Since your tax dollars fund these services, don't hesitate to take advantage of them. A phone call and a sample or two of your soil is all it takes.

The slope of the land is its topography. Every piece of land has some slope. Obviously a steep slope is more of a constraint than a gentle one, but all grade changes offer design opportunities as well. If you have not shown contour lines, but the property does have important grade changes, indicate all these major slopes and mark their high and low points. This is often simply done by marking the tops and bottoms of slopes T.S. (top slope) and B.S. (bottom slope). Where drainage is a problem, it may be helpful to show any major drainage channels as well. Drainageways or runoff channels are usually marked by lack of vegetation, surface gravel or mud banks. They are always obvious after a hard rain. Just remember water runs downhill and they will be easy to spot.

The following checklist of site analysis factors is included here to help you in considering all the possible influences on your land. Many of them are just common sense and not all will pertain to your particular property. So don't be overwhelmed. What is important is that you become aware of those existing conditions which do affect your site, so that you can design with them in mind.

The Existing Conditions Map (sample shown on page 30) is a graphic tool for you to use. It is not a work of art. Don't hesitate to write on it. Scribble a phrase here or there—nice tree, wet spot, whatever. Label any problem areas that exist now or any that you can foresee developing. A recurrent "bald spot" in your lawn or an objectionable view should be labeled as such. All the pertinent factors on the checklist belong on your base map so that you can have a complete graphic record to work with.

NOTE: If your residence is in a townhouse or planned community it is a good idea to construct your base map to include a generous area beyond your immediate boundary, especially if your site borders any form of common ground. Also, any home-owners' association you may belong to should be contacted both as a resource for maps that may have already been prepared and to check for any community restrictions that may exist.

TOPOGRAPHY

SITE ANALYSIS CHECKLIST

Possible Factors to be Shown on the Existing Conditions Map

	Information Needed	Information Obtained	Information not Needed
TOPOGRAPHY			
1. Existing topography			
2. Mark the tops and bottoms of slopes			
3. Degree of slope, either as severe, moderate, minor or in percent grade in extreme cases			
4. Elevation (grade-level) of any major features, if necessary			
DRAINAGE AND SOILS			
1. Directions of drainage with high and low spots			
2. Topsoil—pH			
3. Depth of Soil			
4. Maximum depth of frost (if applicable)			
BOUNDARIES			
1. Property lines			
2. Easements—Buildings, roads, etc.			
3. Rights-of-way			
LEGAL REGULATIONS			
1. Zoning restrictions; such as set-back requirements, etc.			
2. Building by-laws (check with local authorities)			

Information Needed	Information Obtained	Information not Needed

EXISTING VEGETATION

1. Location of all existing trees, size (height and branching spread), good or bad condition
2. Location of shrubs and smaller plants, size (height and spread), good or bad condition

UTILITIES

Location of all utility connections and alignments

SITE AMENITIES (VISUAL SURVEY)

1. Best views, poor views, objectionable views
2. Off-site nuisance, noise, smells, etc.
3. Logical building areas of the site (if you are building)
4. Logical entry and exit points (if you are building)
5. Other particular natural features, e.g., springs, sunken areas, special plants, etc.
6. Orientation to sun, wind
7. Existing driveway, buildings
8. Problem spots
9. Interior arrangement of dwelling (if existing), and proposed interior layout if not yet designed

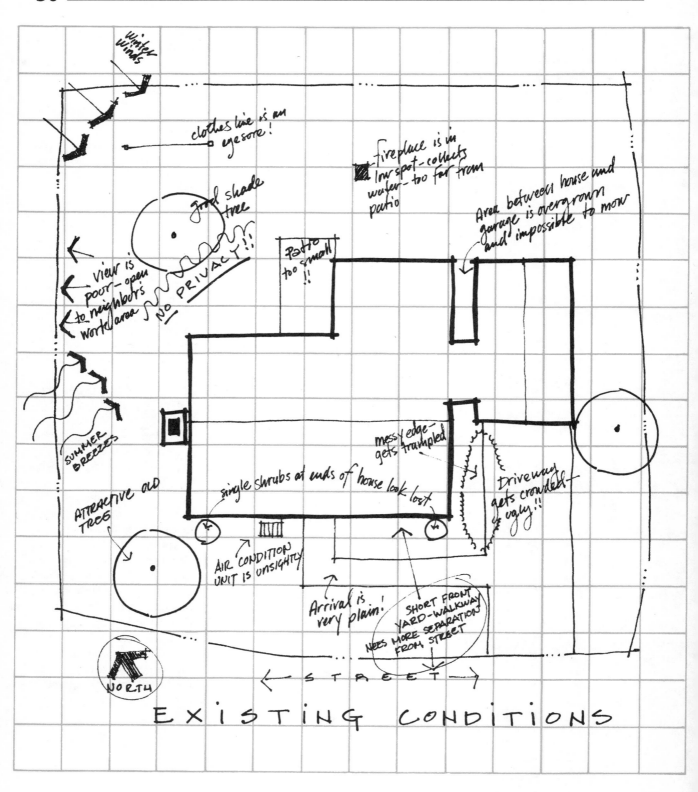

Winter winds

clothes line is an eyesore!

fireplace is in low spot—collects water—too far from patio

Area between house and garage is overgrown and impossible to mow

good shade tree

Patio too small!!

view is poor—open to neighbor's work area

NO PRIVACY!!

messy edge—gets trampled

single shrubs at ends of house look lost

Driveway gets crowded & ugly!!

SUMMER BREEZES

ATTRACTIVE OLD TREES

AIR CONDITION UNIT IS UNSIGHTLY

Arrival is very plain!

SHORT FRONT YARD—WALKWAY NEEDS MORE SEPARATION FROM STREET

NORTH

← S T R E E T →

E X I S T I N G   C O N D I T I O N S

CHAPTER 5

Step 4/Deciding What You Want

Now that you understand the site's existing conditions—what you have to work with—the next step is to decide what you want or need in your home landscape. Is it a children's play area, a spot for a vegetable garden, a storage shed? Which is most important to you? Make a list of all the things you might want. Family discussion is essential here. Different age groups and individuals have their own interests and needs, so everyone should participate to make the list complete.

ASSIGNING PRIORITIES

Once you have a full list, rate the items on a priority basis by assigning a 1, 2, or 3 value to each one depending upon its importance to you. Number one designates a top priority. Which is more important—a car turn-around or the children's play area? Is a vegetable garden a top priority (1) or not? Don't be overwhelmed by the length of the list. The property's constraints, your allowable time allotment, budget considerations, and the priorities you have assigned to each item will quickly weed out the less important ones. Space alone will preclude having everything. Remember too, that your design does not have to be implemented immediately. It can be "phased" over a period of years. Developing your landscape in stages will spread out both the work load and the expenses to fit your time and budget.

EXAMPLE OF A FAMILY'S LIST

Numbered
Importance

1	children's play area
2	vegetable garden
3	flower garden
3	herb garden
1	deck, terrace or both
2	outdoor lighting
1	hard surface area for play, entertaining, etc.
2	car turn-around
1	screen neighbor's garage
3	work/storage shed
3	grill (barbecue)
2	dog pen or leash area
2	extra parking space(s) for guests
1	strong entryway—easy access to front door
2	lawn area suitable for sitting, and grass games— badminton, volleyball, croquet, etc.
1	correct drainage of storm water
2	above-ground swimming pool

To help you zero in your priorities these features may also be considered in terms of the expense, spatial requirements, and maintenance needs. A simple matrix will help.

Family List	Initial Expense	Space Needed	Maintenance Required
Fences	High	Little	Low
Stone Barbecue	High	Medium	Low
Flower Beds	Medium/Low	Medium	High
Dog Pen	Medium/High	High	Medium
Etc.			

CHAPTER 6

Step 5/Diagramming Activity Areas

This is the final step of the planning phase. Dividing the property into activity areas or use zones is a way to further organize your site for designing. Starting with your list's top priorities, assign each item a space according to its rough size requirement and desired location. The placement must obviously reflect the site's existing conditions. Some of these activity areas probably exist now in your landscape and need not be moved, but try not to be restricted too much by what already exists. Many site conditions can be modified. Unfortunately, there are few standard size requirements to go by for these areas. The space needed for parking a Cadillac is larger than that of a Volkswagen. An intimate deck for two people will need less room than a deck used for family entertaining. In general, though, be generous with your size allotments. Refer to Chapter 10 for more information on the sizes of use areas.

As you did with the Existing Conditions Map, either Xerox a copy of your base map or lay a sheet of tracing paper over it. Using a large pencil or Pentel pen, make bold strokes outlining each area. Because the base map is to scale the zones can be located fairly accurately. Step 5 is a preliminary layout, though, and you should not try to be too exact. Designate each zone roughly with circles or oblongs; *don't* follow the grids on the graph paper. Doing that will slow you down and make you think of details too quickly.

WHERE YOU WANT WHAT

MAJOR USE ZONES

There are usually three major use zones in the home landscape: approach, living, and service/work. Each can be broken down further into activity areas.

Approach: driveway, parking, garage, walkways.

Living: terraces, decks, porches, lawns, outdoor play areas, gardens, paths, pools, grills, etc.

Service/Work: storage sheds, trash and garbage areas, working gardens, barns and outbuildings.

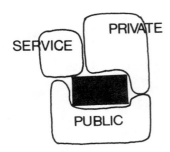

These three major zones are sometimes referred to as public, private, and service zones.

Obviously there is often overlap between these basic areas. A garage may be used as an outdoor work area and as a storage area for trash receptacles, for example. These use overlaps are fine as long as they are clearly understood and delineated where necessary. Most practical plans will include such multipurpose areas. A garbage bin and tool shed built into the garage or a lawn area off the terrace for ball games and party overflow space are simple examples of properly located and related activities. It is the primary use we are concerned with here. In the examples shown the garage is still primarily a service area; the lawn a living area.

When you are diagramming the existing or proposed activity areas remember the importance of both *location* and the *interaction* between them. Keep in mind: adjacency, compatibility of bordering use areas, ease of accessibility, and the interrelatedness of indoor-outdoor spaces. Think about noises, smells, and views. Locating the children's play area next to a street, the driveway, or directly outside the den window would seem questionable. Putting the dog's pen outside the bedroom is another example of poor placement.

Conflicts between activities and placement problems will become apparent as you draw the activity areas on to your plan, such as the playground ending up in a wet spot or walkways becoming too awkward and restrictive. Several arrangements will probably have to be tried before the puzzle pieces begin to fit together.

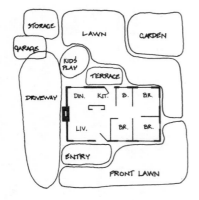

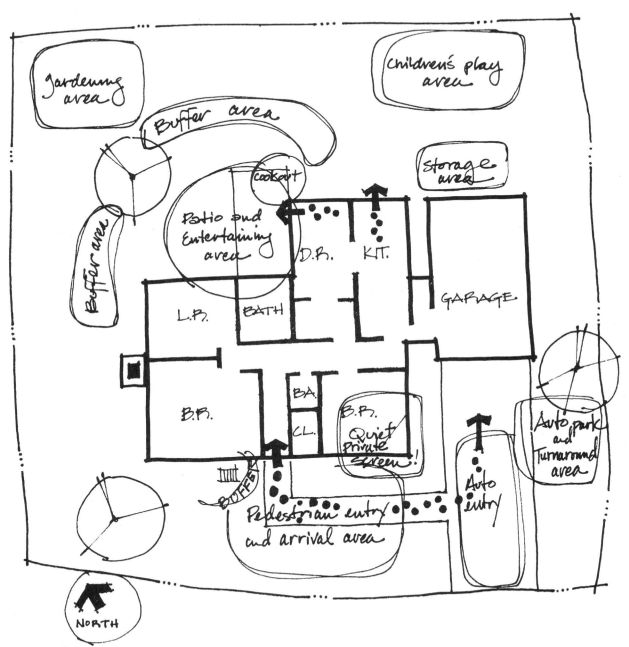

DIAGRAMMING ACTIVITY AREAS

Once you have located the activity areas, add circulation (walks, driveways, paths) and screens and buffers. The latter would include anything that *separates* activity areas. Fences, walls, earthen banks, paving, and trees or shrubs can all be used to separate activities. Many adjacent activities will need to be separated—a rubbish storage area from a deck, for instance—and any separation should be noted on your plan. Circulation shows the movement patterns into and between activity areas. It should be clearly defined and logically placed, just as the activities must be clearly delineated from one another.

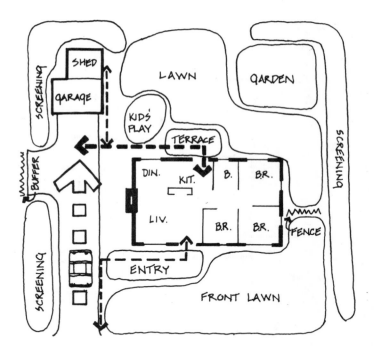

Step 5 is more than planning. It is really the beginning of design. With it you are laying out your property—composing the landscape to fit your needs. If you find that not all of your priority choices fit into the site, go back and weigh them again until the most important stand out. Your design will be well along when you finish this step. So take time to do it well.

CHAPTER 7

The Basics of Design

At this stage you have come to understand the constraints and potentialities of your site (existing conditions), have articulated your goals for its development (priorities), and have assigned general locations for these priorities (activity areas). In other words, you have identified the pieces of your own particular design puzzle and have begun to put them together.

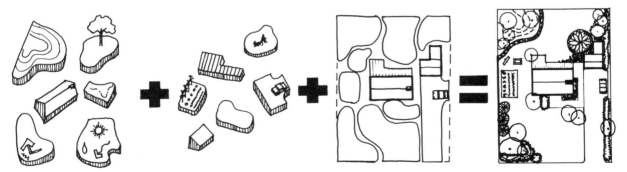

With this, the planning stage has been completed. You have already begun to design: to search for how one puzzle pattern (the actual site) can fit the other (your needs and priorities), without severe damage to either.

Before getting on to Steps 6 and 7, though, it would be worthwhile to review some of the general principles and elements of design and try to get a better understanding of what is involved in residential design. As you go over the following sections, try to apply the material to your plan, particularly as it applies to the overall design. During this time you should be slowly tightening and solidifying the basic scheme. The design details will come later.

THE SEVEN GOALS OF GOOD DESIGN

There are seven general goals for any home landscape plan. Keep them in mind as you weigh the advantages and disadvantages of the various preliminary schemes you develop. They are a classic test for good domestic design. The seven are: privacy, physical comfort, low maintenance, practicality, safety, adaptability and beauty.

Privacy. Almost every household wants at least some private outdoor space. This should be an area to relax in, to be alone, or for informal entertaining. Ideally, it should allow you to sunbathe without feeling like an exhibitionist and have a quiet dinner without having to invite the neighbors. Privacy and seclusion are basic human needs. Try to meet them in your plan.

Physical Comfort: To relax and enjoy the outdoors you have to be physically comfortable. With a little planning you can provide shade from the hot sun, block out strong winds, and lessen noise intrusions.

Low Maintenance. Very few people can afford the time themselves or the professional help required to maintain large, elaborate landscapes. Even among the rich, ostentatious lifestyles are disappearing.

Whether you have several acres or a tiny, urban courtyard, plan for low maintenance. Plant materials that require constant care, pruning, feeding and spraying are generally to be avoided. Be aware of your mower or tractor's maneuverability when you are laying out a lawn. Try to avoid bits and pieces of lawn or garden in your landscape. If the climate is very dry, consider installing a sprinkler system for ease of maintenance, or better yet, create a desert landscape.

Those of you who like to putter around outdoors know that there is always plenty to do. However, there is an important distinction to be made between what you may *want* to do and what you will *have* to do if your landscape requires constant maintenance.

Practicality. To function well, an outdoor space must be clearly organized. Different use areas should be conveniently accessible and sensibly located. Walks must clarify circulation patterns. Allowances should be made for fuel delivery, snow removal, a septic tank truck, and other service vehicles.

Safety. Obviously, your surroundings should be as hazard-free as possible. Steps must be easy to climb and lighting provided where necessary. Sliding glass doors, tree guidewires, and other potential hazards should be easily recognizable. Garden tools will need a child-proof storage area. Be safety conscious in your design.

Adaptability. Not only will shrubs and trees grow, but your own needs will change. Children grow older; you may build a new wing onto your home, or decide you want a pool or a barn. Keep the future in mind. An inflexible plan will eventually defeat itself, because it will be unable to accommodate the changes that time brings.

Incorporating multi-purpose or multi-use areas into your design will help. Yesterday's volleyball court becomes lawn, the children's play area is made over as a garden. Think ahead!

Beauty. Beauty is not the least of these goals. Everyone enjoys and appreciates attractive surroundings. A design should aim to make your property beautiful in every season and from all viewing directions.

PRINCIPLES AND ELEMENTS OF DESIGN

There are no rigid rules for designing. Ultimately, it is a matter of personal taste. However, there are a few, basic design principles and elements worth reviewing. Having an understanding of them will make it much easier to design. These are the building blocks of good design: line, pattern, unity, proportion and scale, balance of accent, and repetition.

Line. The importance of lines lies in their ability to organize a space and control movement. They exist everywhere in the landscape. There are lines formed by roof edges, shrub masses, walkways, topography, house corners and so on, ad infinitum. The most obvious lines are usually found in the existing structure itself. You only have to look for them.

When you begin designing, it often helps to extend a few of these major structural lines out from the house on your plan. These become organizing tools and set up a framework for development. With tracing paper over your plan it is easy to extend the stronger lines formed by a predominant corner, a major door, walls, or other features. These imaginary lines need not connect straight on, but can also come off at a diagonal slant.

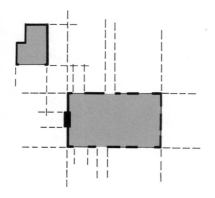

These lines can be the skeleton of a design scheme. As you proceed you will see how they form shapes and create patterns, which in turn will tend to unify the house with its landscape. These shapes and patterns will emerge not only from these extended lines, but in combination with the activity areas and the layout of circulation (e.g., walkways, landings and driveways). Together they can provide an excellent framework for designing.

Pattern. An overall basic pattern is essential for creating a unified, comprehensive design. Such an underlying pattern will normally become apparent in between the extended imaginary lines and/or from the property's existing characteristics, such as slopes and tree masses. It nearly always already exists, particularly in the structure itself. Look for it.

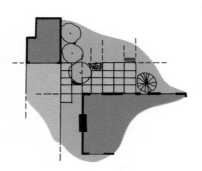

In general, those areas closest to the house require a tighter, more formal pattern reflecting the influence of the building. Further away, the pattern can gradually become looser and more informal in response to the surrounding landscape. Conversely, a small, urban courtyard will generally call for a more defined pattern than a rural dwelling. In all cases the use of a pattern will help to marry the structure to the land.

Unity. A well conceived landscape design is a complete scheme. Every function is understandable and fits comfortably into the overall design. There should be no extraneous, superfluous frills and no "left-over" pieces. Too often, homeowners try to do too much within a limited area and end up with a jumble of unrelated, competing parts. Instead, these exterior spaces and landscape elements should flow into one another, each appearing to be essential to the "wholeness" of the design.

Unity promotes a sense of harmony in a design. Since all the elements are tied together, they seem to belong and are at rest with one another.

There are many ways of introducing unity into a landscape design. The easiest way of unifying a typical piece of property is to enclose it with trees, fences, or hedges—separating it from its surroundings. This has the same effect as framing a painting. It sets it apart as a single entity. A property can also be only partially enclosed and open on one side towards a major feature, such as a view. This unifies the property by focusing all movement and attention in one direction.

Line and pattern also promote a design's unity (harmony) as can the other important design principles: proportion, balance, accent repetition and sequential movement. Here is a way to test your design's unity:

Once your scheme is fairly well developed, take a thick piece of paper and cover up the various parts one at a time. If any of these parts can be thus removed without affecting the whole design, it is probably irrelevant and should be reconsidered. There are exceptions, but usually such a nonessential part will detract from the design's unity.

Proportion and Scale. These two terms are often confused, Proportion refers to the *relationship* between the various landscape elements and scale to the relative *size* of these parts to one another. Together these principles form the backbone of beauty.

All the elements in a design must be in *proportion* to relate well. In other words, the relationship between the dimensions of the different landscape areas—open space, plants, buildings, and paved areas, etc.—should compare favorably with one another. With scale, it is the size of one element which must relate well to the various sizes in its surroundings. In both cases, one element, whether open lawn or a single plant, should not unintentionally overpower and dwarf the other elements in its surroundings.

All of us possess an innate sense of good proportion and scale. Subconsciously we know when something looks right. Pay attention to these subconscious reactions.

Balance—Symmetry and Asymmetry. One reason natural landscapes are so pleasing to us is that they have an inherent stability and balance about them. A natural, undisturbed landscape is at rest. All the elements appear as they should be.

This sense of balance is crucial in landscape design. Every landscape element gives, through its size, shape, color and placement, an impression of weight. Balance is creating equilibrium between two weighted things along a central axis or around a focal point. The weights must appear to be equal.

There are two ways to achieve this desirable sense of balance. The easier and more familiar method is symmetrical balance. This is traditionally the formal means of reaching equilibrium. Here, similar elements are placed on either side of an axis line or central point creating equal weights.

With asymmetrical balance, the elements on either side of the axis line or central point may be quite different in size and shape, but give the appearance of equilibrium through careful placement. This is a more informal, naturalistic method and the sense of balance it conveys is subtler and more difficult to achieve.

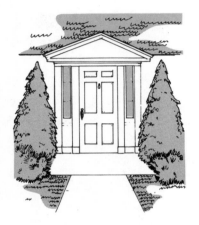

Symmetrical balance

Formal, symmetrical balance on a grand scale is impractical on most homesites today for economic reasons. Moreover, it is not usually compatible with contemporary architecture, typical lot sizes, or our evolving, more informal, lifestyles. Therefore, asymmetrical balance is generally preferable, particularly in new home construction. It is more difficult to do well, though, and great care must be taken in developing an asymmetrical balance.

Concerning formal and informal styles, most homes today quite correctly use both in their landscapes. Don't feel restricted to one or the other exclusively. It would be quite understandable if one area, especially near the house, were more formal in nature than another area farther from the dwelling.

Asymmetrical balance

Accent and Repetition. Attention to the above principles can all be overdone. Too much unity or balance breeds monotony.

Accent and repetition can alleviate this and heighten the attractiveness of your design.

Accents are highlights. They can be either incidental or climactic in nature. They increase the viewer's interest and encourage the eye to move from one point to another. Well executed, these eye movements add an underlying sense of rhythm and sequence to a scheme.

Incidental accents take advantage of contrasting colors, textures and shapes. Something as simple as putting a tree into a hedgerow can provide an accent. Slightly modulating a space, changing the direction or character of a major line, and using garden accessories are other examples. A carefully placed birdbath, bench or windchime can add to a scheme's interest. Water features and sculpture are rich additions too. But be careful. Too many accessories, particularly if they are of dubious quality, can result in a cluttered look.

Most successful landscapes include an area (or areas) towards which the design and plant materials build up. These more highly finished areas are called climaxes or focal points. They are nearly always located along or terminate major axial lines and are closely related to the principles of line and pattern. Climax accents give movement, direction and unity to a design. Traditionally, they have been the means of formally terminating primary axial lines. All such lines have to be ended appropriately and climaxes are the accepted method. In a formal scheme, a major climax may include special features such as a reflecting pond or garden wall. A secondary axis line can be ended much less dramatically.

Repetition. Used with restraint, repetition similarly heightens interest. When a landscape element or principle such as a line, shape, pattern, or planting group is used several times, repetition is introduced. For example, the basic shape of a rectangular terrace could be repeated in a low, bordering hedge and then again in planting beds below and beyond the terrace. Similarly, the lines of a garden path can be repeated in adjacent, parallel plantings. Equally spaced like plantings have the same effect.

In general, dominant shapes in the landscape should be echoed by repetition in the surrounding design. Squares and rectangles relate better and belong within like shapes. The same

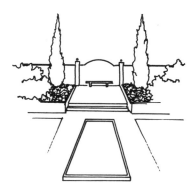

A major axial focal point in a formal garden

elevation

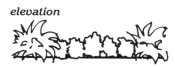

plan view

elevation

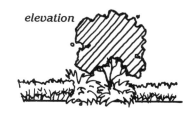

plan view

Secondary focal points can be much less dramatic, but must still terminate and receive the axial lines.

is true of circular or oblique shapes. The repeated elements need not be identical, however. What is important is that the essence or impression of similarity is conveyed.

PLANTS AND EARTHFORMS AS SPATIAL TOOLS

Too often plant materials are used solely as decorative afterthoughts and earthforms purposefully neglected in favor of flat sites. This is unfortunate because both are basic landscape tools for shaping outdoor space.

Plants should first be located and chosen primarily to fulfill certain functions—as separators, accents, background, or windscreens. Their obvious aesthetic appeal is supportive and secondary. Landforms such as mounds and terraces are also functional landscape tools. If one reconsiders the ground plane as literally an outdoor floor, the potential of earthforms is more readily apparent. While the specifics of plant composition, plant selection and grading will be covered in Chapters 11 and 13, this is an appropriate time, while you are solidifying your design schemes, to emphasize the importance of plant materials and earthforms as spatial tools.

Every homeowner should consider using plants as structural elements in the landscape. They can provide scale, emphasize or minimize land form changes, control circulation, provide buffers and, most of all, define spaces.

In this early stage it is not necessary to assign specie types to the trees and shrubs you use to serve spatial functions. Just indicate them as circles on your plan and perhaps mark them as deciduous or evergreen and as either large trees, small trees, shrubs, or ground-cover. You should be getting far enough along to know generally the size and shape required to fulfill the plants' function. In the plant material chapter we will show how to

PLANTS CAN:

Provide scale and shade

Accentuate or soften topography

Direct movement

Separate activities

Enclose and define spaces

Provide privacy

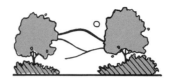

Frame views

Reduce glare

Act as a windbreak and noise buffer

Lead the eye and emphasize special features

Act as insulating material

Soften architecture and help to relate the building to the land

translate this information into a planting plan with appropriate species for your climate and site.

Earthforms can form structural landscape elements as well. Sculptured slopes, mounds and bowls can screen objectionable views, buffer noise, and act as space separators. Levels or terraces are one of the best means to separate activities since they segregate areas through grade changes, not enclosure. Wherever feasible, level changes should be considered to enhance the garden. Steep slopes also have spatial qualities, directing all movement—physically and visually—out from the slope. Homeowners seem to have an almost automatic aversion to slopes on their sites. While admittedly somewhat difficult to work with, slopes and level changes offer numerous design potentials. Their use as accents and their ability to attract and focus attention are too often overlooked. A climax or focal point will be much more effective, for example, if it is slightly raised above the surrounding landscape. Indeed, even small level changes can

EARTHFORMS CAN:

Physically and visually direct movement

Buffer and screen noise, wind and undesirable views

Separate activities

Create space

dramatically heighten a design's interest by breaking up the dull-
ness of a perfectly level site. In the mistaken rush to "correct" his
lot by flattening it, many a homeowner has destroyed the most
desirable characteristic of his property. Particularly if your site
already has noticeable topographic changes, try to view them as
assets and incorporate them positively into your design. They will
add interest and variety to your landscape.

CHAPTER 8

Tapping the Imagination

Imagination is the facility to form ideas and mental images. It involves idea-stretching and creative seeing. All of us employ visual thinking daily without being aware of it. Passing on a freeway or moving a large piece of furniture from one room to another are both examples of the mind using visual images to complete a task. The imagination sees and anticipates the necessary movements which the mind can then accept or reject. Design ideas can be mentally explored in much the same way.

Actually, you have already been called upon to use visualizing powers in recognizing the existing problems and assets of your land. Being able to visualize potentials—a wet spot as a pond, a view hidden behind trees, or "seeing" how a proposed planting might look—is extremely important in designing. Your imagination also allows you to take the third dimension—height—into consideration. Since your design work will be done primarily on a two-dimensional map, you will have to rely largely on your imagination to provide you with the crucial third dimension.

Visualizing is hard for those of us who do not consciously use our imaginations on a day-to-day basis. Amateur landscapers often make mistakes because they neglect the third dimension or have been unable to "see" what a proposed mass of shrubs, a new fence, or other features would look like in the landscape. Being able to visualize brings with it a degree of design freedom. It allows you to test a design with your mind's eye.

LEARNING TO VISUALIZE

EXERCISES IN VISUALIZATION

Two ways of improving your inherent imaginative powers are practice and using graphic techniques, like sketching. The three visualizing exercises below are included to give you a little practice in imagination-stretching. They are meant to jar your imagination awake. How well you succeed with each one is unimportant.

EXERCISE #1:

Wherever you are in your home, sit back a moment and relax. Be conscious of the wall directly ahead of you. Look at it. Keeping any foreground furniture in focus, slowly dissolve this wall. See through it. Since you know what is on the other side, this is easy to do. If there is another interior wall beyond it, dissolve that one as well until you can mentally "see" outside of your house. Try this several times if necessary. Using your imagination, feel the wind come in where the wall used to be. Smell and hear the outdoors as if the wall was truly not there.

EXERCISE #2:

Again, relax. Sit quietly and close your eyes for this exercise. Imagine yourself in front of your house. Orient yourself to the surroundings. Now, very slowly, begin to walk around the house. Look at everything. If you find yourself skipping ahead from one spot to another, begin again. Buried in your memory is a mental picture of every foot around your house. Call it up to the surface. Be sure to go slowly. When you have succeeded in going slowly all the way around, open your eyes again.

EXERCISE #3:

Ideally you should be outside for this exercise. Once more relax. Slowly project yourself above your property, at first only a few feet, then higher so that more and more of the site comes into view. Look down and orient yourself to the land as seen from above. This is the same view as your two-dimensional plan. This imaginative projecting of yourself is hard, but it does offer valuable new insights as to how your landscape looks from a new perspective.

EXERCISE #4:

For this last exercise, bring out your base map or your existing conditions map and set it down in front of you. Relax. Choose one small problem area on your plan. Focus in on it. When the area's plan (two-dimensional) view is imbedded on your mind, close your eyes. Mentally project yourself to be standing directly in front of the area. Be aware of the third dimension, the surrounding height of things. Look at the problem spot for a few moments. Now *change* one of the shapes in your imaginary view. Now a color. Finally, change the problem area to what you eventually want it to be like. What does your proposed design for it look like? Does it work?

This last is by far the most difficult of the exercises. It is also the most important as it asks that you visualize in three dimensions a proposed change. Try this a few times.

Another easy way to start thinking in the third dimension is to look upon your outdoor space as a room. The lawn and paved areas are the floor—fences, shrubs, tree silhouettes, a neighboring building could form the walls—with the canopy of overhead trees and finally the sky becoming the ceiling. Remembering this analogy—your outdoor space as a room—will help you later in designing the landscape.

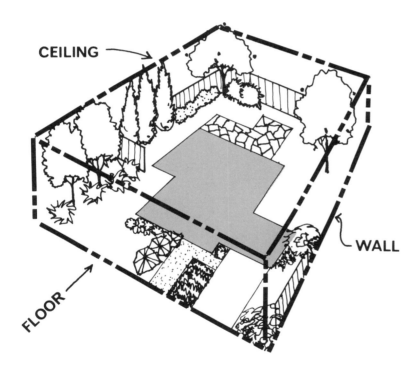

CEILING

WALL

FLOOR

It helps to be able to put design ideas on paper quickly. This is particularly true in the early stages of developing a design scheme. When working with tracing paper over a base map, your tentative design lines should be loose, quick, and messy. Do not be concerned with their artistic value. Early designs are like doodles. These scribbles are not meant to be exact, neat, or

**SKETCHES
AND DOODLES**

beautiful. They are for exploring ideas. Almost everyone has heard stories about architects scribbling their inspirations on restaurant tablecloths. There is a lesson here. Don't begin designing with tight, thin lines. You will have more fun, get better results and work much faster if you relax and draw with loose, free strokes.

Use sweeping, bold lines to try out several schemes. It does not matter one bit if these doodles are incomprehensible to anyone but you. Only when a design scheme begins to show promise should you begin to clean it up, tightening the lines and making it more accurate. It is a foregone conclusion that a lot of tracing paper will end up in the trash basket!

For the doodle stage of design, you may find a grease pencil or laundry marker a far better tool than a regular pencil. Using a large marker of some kind will force you to loosen up and be bolder with your lines.

Loose, quick, messy, but helpful.

Slide Projection. One other technique that allows you to see what you are designing uses a slide projector. This slide method is useful for testing a specific design "in place." First, you will have to have taken slides of the particular problem areas you are working on. These can be projected onto any accessible wall. Then place a sheet of thin tracing paper over the projected picture and tape it to the wall. Now you can roughly sketch your design ideas right into their actual surroundings.

This method is especially good for testing proportion and scale in your design. In fact, you can design as you sketch over the projected picture. The number of ideas you can pursue is only limited by the amount of tracing paper you have. If you try it, get yourself in a comfortable position to sketch as your raised arm will tire quickly.

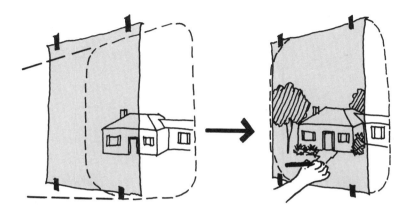

Using Photographs. Photographs can be used in a similar way. You can either sketch right onto the picture itself or lay a small piece of tracing paper over it. Polaroids are especially well suited for this since the picture is developed immediately. You can get up, go take a shot of exactly the area you are working on and come back with a photographic reproduction to design from.

CHAPTER 9

Step 6/Designing the Overall Scheme

The design review in Chapter 7 was meant to guide you in the right direction and help you to avoid the more common mistakes. The building blocks discussed there are essential in creating a good landscape plan. If the basics we reviewed are followed in organizing your overall scheme, the major parts of the design plan will be on solid ground. Later, the specific details will fall naturally into place. Refer back to these basics frequently as you work on your overall scheme.

With Step 5 you have identified and analyzed the site's existing conditions, your priorities and needs and the general location of the various activity areas. Now, in Step 6, this information is translated into a loose, comprehensive development scheme. An overall scheme is really a rough design. Based on the information gained so far, you should be able to create a *rough* overall scheme. Several rough drafts will probably have to be tried out before one is settled upon. The merits and difficulties of each trial scheme should be weighed in creating your finished overall scheme.

In Step 6 it is important to design a rough scheme that works in terms of circulation, separation of activities, and topography. Don't become prematurely concerned with its aesthetic qualities. And remember that only when you have completed such a scheme should you begin to concentrate on the details of each landscape component (e.g., materials, final dimensions and construction methods).

Paying attention to the following section on Common Design

Problems will make this step easier. Your overall scheme should
be as nearly complete as the one shown here.

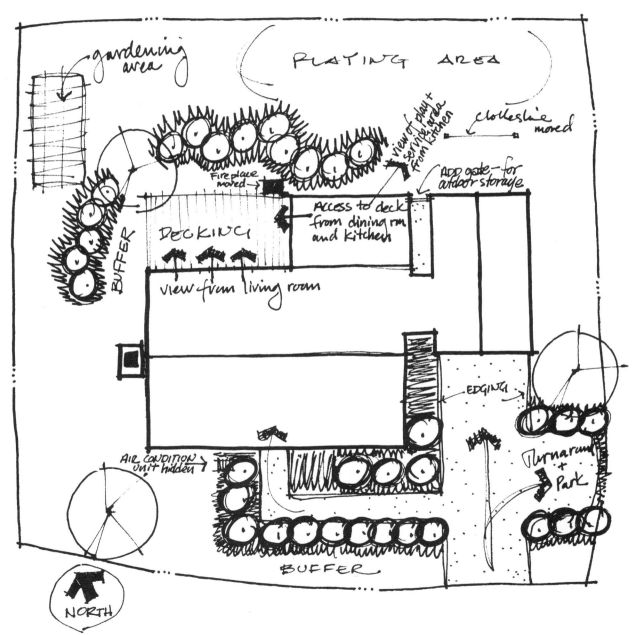

OVERALL SCHEME

COMMON DESIGN PROBLEMS

The nature of design is such that though it can be explained in a linear manner, as a series of steps, it is also somewhat circular in practice. By this I mean that you must go back and check and recheck your design. Right up to the end you should try to improve the fit of the design's puzzle pieces. This rechecking of the design is particularly important. Conflicts and potential problems can still be caught at this stage without too great a waste of time. One good way to spot mistakes in the overall scheme stage is to check them against the list of common design problems described below.

1. An Overly Complex Design. It is tempting to use far too many different materials and plant types and to have too many things going on. Don't clutter up your property. The best plans, especially for beginners, are simple and straightforward. Remember that complex designs are costly, too.

2. Inflexible ideas. Holding on to fixed, inflexible ideas while you try to design is self-defeating. To design well, your mind must be receptive to new ideas. Rigid ideas will blind you to the design clues of your site. In the end your preconceived pet idea may prove to be correct, but allow it to prove itself through the design process first.

3. Overlooking the Obvious. Familiarity blinds us. This is why it is important to take a fresh look at your property. That huge, beautiful tree you no longer really see, much as you no longer hear the ticking of a bedside clock, may provide the logical setting for a terrace. Look for the obvious.

4. Jumping Ahead of Yourself. So often homeowners will worry about details in one area without having completed an overall scheme—for example, deciding on a specific brick pattern for a walk before having located the walk itself sensibly within the design. Details like this must come *after* the overall scheme has been worked out, not before. So follow the steps of the design process. Go back and recheck yourself, yes, but don't jump *ahead* of the steps.

5. Not Tapping the Imagination Enough. Everyone has an active imagination. Use yours and give it free rein. Think of as many solutions to the problem as possible. Part of the fun of designing is that even the slightly crazy thoughts should be considered. Sometimes they end up being the best.

6. Neglect of the Third Dimension. This is the downfall of many designs. The third dimension has two meanings here. One refers to the undulations in your property's topography. If the slopes and grade changes are overlooked, the results can be disastrous. The other is visualizing height as a design component. What will something look like in place? To know you have to consider the third dimension. It is all too easy to forget the importance of height when you are concentrating on a flat, two-dimensional drawing.

7. Not Establishing Priorities. Without a clear list of priorities you cannot plan what you need or want on your landscape. Step 4 is crucial. There is no way to judge if a landscape plan is successful without knowing what functions it was meant to have.

8. Artistic Vanity. There is a tendency to pay far too much attention to producing an *artistically* pleasing design on paper. These plans are design tools only! They are not meant for the National Gallery. The success of a design depends on how it looks and functions in the landscape, not on how it might look framed.

9. Overlooking the Site's Innate Characteristics. The land itself strongly dictates the direction a design should take. Again and again, homeowners ignore these clues and try, unsuccessfully, to impose their own ideas of how it should look. A successful landscape design is responsive to the problems and potentials of its site.

10. Lack of Adaptability. A plan that does not foresee and allow for change is dead. Children grow up; small trees get large; lifestyles alter. Anticipate these changes. If a foreseeable change—such as a new wing on the house—would totally destroy the continuity of your plan, reconsider it.

11. Adding "Cute" or "False" Elements. Be very careful when including sculpture and ceramic details in your plan. An obviously cheap garden accessory will lower the quality of your entire design. Similarly, every element should have a clear, apparent function. Walkways should go somewhere and fences and walls should actually separate functions. A trellis that does not and probably could not support vines is a questionable addition to the landscape. Avoid purposeless elements.

12. Choosing Plant Species Too Quickly. In domestic landscape design it is essential that the location and use of plant materials—as separators, accents, or for other purposes—be determined first, before decisions are made on the most appropriate type of plant for the job. Decide what you want the plant for, think about its aesthetic qualities, and then look for the desired species.

13. Being Overly "Cost-conscious." Financial constraints are real. Nevertheless, design generously at first and then count costs. With a completed design you are in a much better position to cut back—based on your priorities for development—and to determine what the total expenditure will be. Spending a little more on a key feature will also give your landscape an elegance and luxury that you cannot achieve if you have cut back everywhere in your design.

14. Being Overly Subtle and Timid. Generally, it is far better to be bold and strong in a design. The lines and spaces should be very definite. Plant growth and time itself will inevitably soften the landscape. Even the harshest plans on paper become muted when they are in place. The entire environment with its textures, colors, and other features will soften the rigidness of a design. So be bold!

15. Allocating Insufficient Space. Be sure to set aside an adequate amount of land to accommodate each outdoor activity. Some things, such as a car turn-around, have general size requirements to go by (see Chapter 10), while others are a matter of judgement. Remember, though, that outdoor spaces should be larger than corresponding indoor spaces because of their context—the great outdoors. Where a 15 foot by 20 foot room may seem fine indoors, these same dimensions would be dwarfed outside the house. Be generous in your space allocations. Your yard is not a place to feel cramped in.

16. Poor Organization. To function well the landscape plan must organize a property efficiently and eliminate conflicts between activities. Walkways should be clearly indicated and should lead to and from specific points. Different, competing activity areas—the dog's pen and the vegetable garden, the terrace seating area and the rubbish bin, or the children's play area and the roadway—should not be located next to one another. If, in the interest of space, they must be adjacent, separate them visually and physically with a landscape element such as a fence, a grade change, or plantings. Examine your overall design for any similar potential conflicts.

These are typical *overall design* problems. The common pitfalls of planting design such as overcrowding, colors, and composition are dealt with separately.

CHAPTER 10

Getting Down to Specifics: Site Features

Now that your overall landscape scheme has been completed, it is time to go on to the detailed development of the different areas. Now you can get specific. What materials are best suited to your design? Should the walk be brick or gravel? What shape should you choose for the deck? The easiest way to do this is to treat each of the major landscape elements individually—remembering, of course, their context in your overall design. Everything should relate harmoniously.

As you read along, use this new information to go back and check your design. Keep solidifying your ideas. Get more explicit. The location, common problems and materials of each of the major man-made landscape components will be discussed.

CONSTRUCTION MATERIALS

A few words on construction materials in general need to be said here. There are many reasons for choosing a particular material. Durability, ease of installation, cost and maintenance factors name only a few. Two other considerations should be kept in mind: the material's building characteristics and its expression.

By its nature, every material has distinctive characteristics that render it suitable for different purposes. For instance, the form and shape of a gravel walk can be quite different from that of a brick walk because of the particular characteristics of each material. All building materials—wood, gravel, concrete, brick—have these inherent qualities that dictate how they can be used and what forms and shapes they can take. These same qualities give any particular material its individual feeling or expression. Random-width fieldstone conveys a different impression from mortared, cut stone. Wood is warmer than concrete; brick is more formal than gravel.

Keep these differences in mind when you are choosing building materials. The material dictates not only the form and shape of the object to be constructed, but also determines the impression or feeling that the object will evoke.

DRIVEWAYS

The driveway strongly influences the design and appearance of any dwelling's public area. On a small site, it can cover and dominate the entire setting of the home. Since it forms the main approach to most houses (except in dense urban situations), the driveway must relate directly to the dwelling's main entry. A well designed drive should serve as an attractive and accessible approach to the home, connecting the front door with the garage and/or parking area.

Because it takes up so much space, tends to dominate the public side of the home and is expensive to construct, a driveway's placement and construction deserves careful consideration. The key is determining how to best site it for convenience and safety without wasting space and disrupting other activities. Normally, driveways should not be winding, long, or steep. Such drives are extremely costly, and they are difficult to back out of. Parking should be a safe distance from the street and close enough to the house for easy access. Ideally, driveways should include a turn-around and at least one parking space for visitors and deliveries. The space thus given over to the drive has multiple benefits, not the least of which is the safety of entering traffic head-on as opposed to backing out into it.

On a medium-sized flat lot with a drive of less than eighty feet, a straight approach is usually best. A house on a steep grade from the street requires a longer, curved drive to maintain a safe, maximum grade level. A steep drive should also have level transition areas, the length of a car or more, where it meets the street and near the house. On a large site where a long drive is required, some gentle curves are acceptable and serve to increase

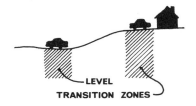

LEVEL
TRANSITION ZONES

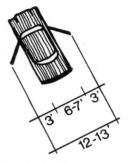

If the people in this car are to be able to step out comfortably onto pavement, a driveway width of twelve feet will be needed.

interest. Any curves, however, should respond somehow to the landform, the vegetation masses, and the visibility of the house itself. Such long driveways offer classic possibilities for making the approach a pleasant experience.

For obvious cost reasons, contractors usually build drives at the absolute minimum width of six to eight feet. A ten- to twelve-foot width is preferable because it allows the driver and passengers to open their doors and step out onto pavement instead of onto shrubs and grass. In newer homes the driveway often serves as the walkway to the house. If the drive is to serve this double purpose, a twelve- to fourteen-foot width is strongly recommended for the same reasons.

Turnaround dimensions

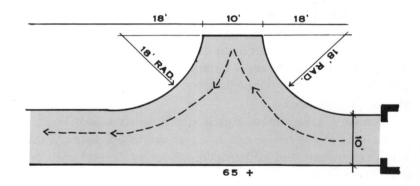

DRAINAGE

a: Ditch and gutter and crown. Drainage is essential on a drive to avoid icing and wet spots. Crowning the drive forces water to either side and away.

b: Driveway "cut" situation with hillside ditch for intercepting run-off

c: Minimum crown on a twelve-foot drive is three inches; eight-foot drive two inches.

d: Pitched drive where runoff is forced to one side and down or off the drive.

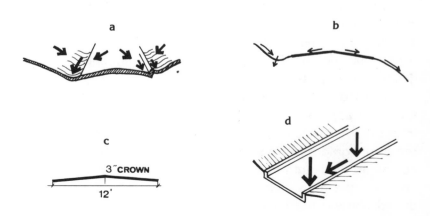

Serious consideration should be given to including a turn-around and/or parking areas, which allow easy vehicular movement without the constant annoyance of having to play "musical cars" every time someone wants to leave. There is a safety factor, too, since a turn-around will lessen the possibility of accidents happening in the drive by allowing head-on access to the street.

The width and construction of the driveway and turn-around obviously depend on the anticipated usage. If delivery trucks, particularly oil and septic tank trucks, will be using it, a heavier roadbed will be needed.

The most widely used building materials for residential driveways are asphalt, concrete, crushed rock and gravel. Concrete and asphalt are quite expensive, but are relatively wear-resistant and have a finished, crisp look to them. Crushed stone and gravel are cheaper. Crushed stone, particularly if it is well laid, will form a compact, long-lasting surface. For more information on concrete and gravel paving turn to the heading "Hard Surface" in this chapter.

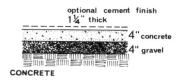

Concrete surface

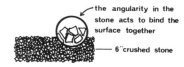

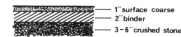

Crushed stone and asphalt surface

DRIVEWAY PLACEMENT

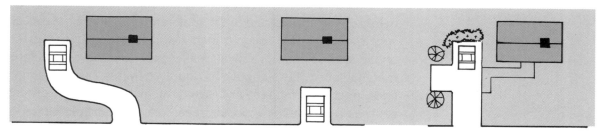

Excessive curves on a flat site are expensive, unrelated to the lot's topography, and difficult to maneuver.

Dominates and divides property.

Turnaround increases maneuverability and handles overflow parking. Planting defines and separates vehicular traffic from other activities.

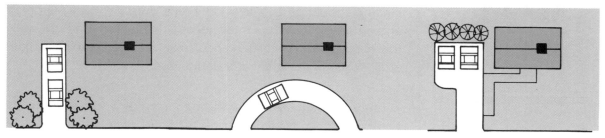

Too narrow, "musical cars" problem. Trees at the end of the drive dangerously obstruct vision.

On a small site curves or loops take up far too much space and are prohibitively expensive.

Extra wide drive doubles as sidewalk and allows parking space for second car.

The arrangement of the house, garage and driveway can be used to create interesting spaces.

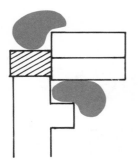 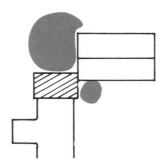 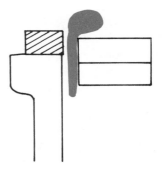

ENTRYWAYS AND WALKS

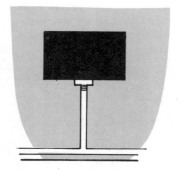

Every home needs a pleasant, obvious entrance. The entryway should be reinforced with architectural and landscape elements to be clear and inviting to the visitor. There are several ways to heighten the importance of the main entrance. Plant masses and specimens can be used to clarify and frame it. Landings can enhance the sense of arrival. Making the landing of a different material from the sidewalk is doubly helpful. Tasteful lighting adds nocturnal interest and safety at night. Vertical elements, such as benches, lampposts, trees, fences, and trellises can all call attention to the entry, too.

The path to the main door should be wide enough for two people to walk side by side. Four feet is considered the absolute minimum and a five- or six-foot width is strongly recommended. Any steps or ramps along the sidewalk or leading up to the landing should be equally wide. Steps must be clearly apparent and emphasized with plants and/or lighting. Long, narrow walks that divide the property and end in skinny steps are to be avoided at all costs as unsightly and dangerous.

Entry Garden. As is true throughout your whole scheme, the entryway should relate in its design and its materials to the architecture of the house and to the natural surroundings. It may help to think of the area leading up to and immediately around the main entrance as the entry garden. Choose plants that are attractive year-round and hardy species that require no special pampering. There are two reasons for choosing hardy plants: (1) roof overhangs often prevent sun and rainwater from always reaching the plants and, (2) in cold climates, shoveling the walks usually buries them under heavy snow piles. Snow and ice falling from the roofs can further aggravate this problem.

Always separate the automobile itself from the main entry, if only by a few feet. In schemes where pedestrians will approach solely from the drive, it is important that some transition and delineation take place. You may wish to leave at least a three- or four-foot wide strip between the walkway and the house. Preferably, this strip should be even wider and thickly planted with shrubs and/or groundcover, *not* grass. Gravel, river stones, mulches and groundcovers can all be used in this isolated planting bed for low maintenance.

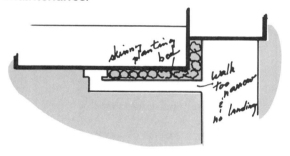 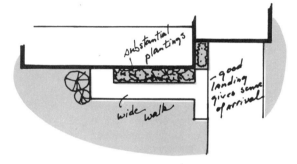

Do not automatically plant a row of identical evergreens along your foundation! This entry treatment is uninteresting and banal. It is far more interesting to use a mixture of plant sizes and shapes, both deciduous and coniferous, and plant them in

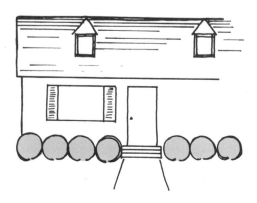 

groups or masses. Remember that they should have an overall design purpose first and should not just be "bargain" plant material randomly placed.

UNINVITING

* house foundation too high
* too many steps needed
* steps are too narrow
* no landing provided
* plantings inadequate

BETTER

* foundation grading raised to lower house and necessitate only two steps
* wide landing for sense of arrival and comfort
* plantings complementary

FRONT LAWNS

Traditionally in this country front lawns have been maintained for the benefit of the public and little used by the owners themselves. A tremendous amount of energy is put into presenting a well kept front for passersby. This often amounts to sacrificing a part of your property for the momentary pleasure of passing motorists. On small properties, at least, doing so is an unjustifiable waste of precious space. Indeed, the front yard as we traditionally know it is really an anachronism left over from the 19th-century English landscape school that was rendered largely disfunctional when it became miniaturized on small, suburban lots. *You are not bound by this tradition.* Don't hesitate to utilize the front yard, then, if that is compatible with your scheme. Especially if the street traffic is heavy and annoying, feel free to enclose the front of your property. A fence or plantings will accomplish this. One of the nicest front lawns I can recall was actually taken up completely by a carefully tended vegetable garden. True, your hidebound neighbors may frown at first, but it could also start a new gardening trend in your area.

TERRACES, PATIOS AND DECKS

At least one large, outdoor living area is always desirable. This "exterior room" increases the living space of a house and is ideal for relaxing, entertaining and other assorted family activities. It should be located off of a convenient entrance for easy access and is best designed as an extension of an indoor room, usually the living room or den. If a large window or sliding glass doors face onto this main terrace, so much the better; they will visually tie the indoor and outdoor spaces together. Sometimes it is advisable to add a picture window for just that purpose.

Terraces, decks and patios all serve to anchor the home to the land in the same manner that plant materials can. They offer welcome, comfortable outdoor space and provide a transition between the dwelling and the landscape. Many homes can incorporate several successfully into their design: an entry landing, a small intimate bedroom terrace, a kitchen patio, and a main entertaining deck.

The main difference between terraces, patios and decks is that the first two are at the ground level and hard-surfaced, while decks are wooden and raised above the ground level. Decks are therefore used predominantly on sites with steep slopes where a level terrace or patio would be impractical. In all cases they should be designed to relate well with the dwelling's architecture and should be constructed of harmonious materials.

Proper Location. The primary factors in determining the proper location for these outdoor rooms is ease of accessibility and compatibility with the adjacent indoor rooms. Strong consideration should also be given to taking advantage of views, shade and sun. In temperate climes, the southeast corner of a home is often recommended for maximum morning sun and partial afternoon sun. The sunless, northern side of the home is always the least desirable.

FACTORS IN LOCATION

sun & shade

winds

views

DEN compatibility with & access to indoor room
TERRACE

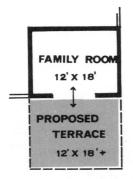

Another terrace size rule of thumb is that ideally the outdoor space should be as large or larger than the adjacent indoor room.

Size. The main terrace or deck ought to be large enough to accommodate several people comfortably, with room for outdoor furniture and barbecues, and it should be constructed to withstand intensive use. As a general rule an area of 8 feet by 8 feet or sixty-four square feet is required for each member of the family. With a large family this quickly becomes a sizeable area; nevertheless, it is usually better to be on the large side. A small, cluttered terrace is not only self-defeating; it is expensive to expand later.

Drainage. Proper drainage is crucial with ground-level terraces and patios. Large, poorly drained, hard-surfaced flat areas will tend to puddle and be rendered useless for long periods. A slope or grade of one to three percent should always be built into the terrace leading away from the house. In northern climates, they will also usually require a firm foundation to withstand winter frost heaves.

Shape. The shape you choose will depend on the home's architecture, the planned development of the rest of the yard and, of course, your personal taste. Generally squares and rectangles are easier to work with and they always relate well with traditional building forms. Interesting and easily buildable shapes can be developed using a simple module system. Starting with 2 feet by 2 feet or 4 feet by 4 feet squares, you can design numerous combinations.

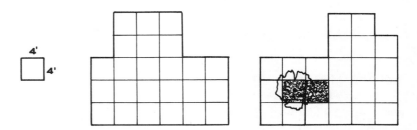

Curvilinear forms can be very pleasing, but are harder to design well and more difficult to build. If you have decided to have a

Try to incorporate and take advantage of special features—a tree through a deck or a natural rock outcropping within a terrace adds appeal.

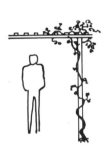  

Giving your terrace or deck a ceiling will make it a more intimate, comfortable place. Trellises, arbors, tree canopies and awnings are all excellent for this.

The area under raised decks can be unsightly. If the deck is high, as in example A, the area underneath can be either paved as a covered terrace or possibly planted. With a lower deck the underneath may be hidden with plantings or the soil stabilized with rip-rap.

free-form terrace be sure to use graceful, gradual curves. Organic forms should clearly respond to adjacent landforms, flowing up to or around natural obstacles like trees or large rocks. Regardless of the shape you choose, always avoid narrow, tight, purposeless spaces and sharp angles.

Steps do two things in the landscape: they allow comfortable passage from one level to another; they connect and tie together different areas and direct circulation. They can vary from narrow and steep to broad and ramp-like. The construction, design, and the material(s) chosen depend largely on their purpose and overall landscape context.

STEPS

Materials. The material chosen should convey the relative importance of the steps and should fit in comfortably with its surroundings. A set of steps leading to the main entry calls for a stronger treatment than minor steps in the garden. Similarly, concrete or cut-stone steps would be out of context in an informal, woodland setting. Wood and dry-laid stone are usually considered informal whereas concrete, mortared brickwork, and cut stone are formal.

Limiting your choice of step construction materials to those already being used elsewhere in the landscape is recommended. A few materials repeated in different ways throughout the landscape always promote unity and harmony in a design.

Dimensions. The primary criteria in step construction is the ease with which they can be climbed. Fortunately a great deal of research has been done in step design. All steps have two components: the *tread*—the flat part you walk on; and the *riser*—the vertical part on which each step rests.

Beauty, safety and comfort in step construction depend on the relationship between the tread and riser. The size of each can vary within limits. The accepted rule is that two risers plus one tread should equal 27 inches. $2R + T = 27''$.

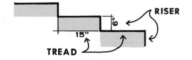

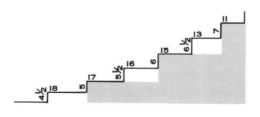

Some tread/riser combinations

Once a set of dimensions is decided upon for a flight of steps, their relationship must remain constant. An unannounced change in either the tread or riser will send you and your guests for a fall. The same tread to riser relationship should extend to adjacent flights of steps as well.

A four foot minimum in width is suggested for most steps and five or six feet is even better. Five feet is absolutely necessary if two people are to use the steps simultaneously. Occasionally far wider steps are called for. A few, very wide steps off a terrace, for instance, can be used for reasons of scale. They add an expansive elegance that is hard to surpass.

These dimensions are purposely larger than those commonly employed on indoor steps. The grand scale of the outdoors and a relaxed garden atmosphere calls for generous dimensions.

In designing steps, it is usually better to mold the slope to fit the most comfortable steps than vice versa. The slope can be shaped by either cutting into the bank or filling out the slope.

The best step design need not necessarily follow the shortest route between the two levels to be negotiated. Steps can zigzag or curve across the slope as well as run straight up it. When many steps are required, landings should be used to break up both the climb and visual impact of seemingly endless steps. Also, *try never to use only one step.* Two or three are much safer and more aesthetically pleasing.

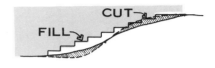

Construction details for brick, concrete and railroad tie steps

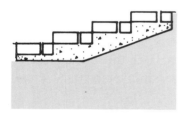

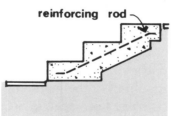

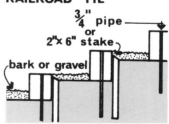

RAMPS

Ramps are the other means of getting from one level to another. They can be used in place of steps and/or to accommodate any handicapped persons among your family and friends. Occasionally ramps are suggested for heart attack victims as well, since they exert less physical strain than stairs.

Wood and concrete are the most common ramp construction materials and an 8 percent grade is usually recommended. Ten percent is acceptable over short distances and in extreme circumstances. Ramps are not space efficient. An 8 percent ramp with a two-foot rise will require a length of twenty-four feet. (8% =1':12') By comparison, steps can negotiate that rise easily over four feet.

Nevertheless, ramps are worth considering because they allow for the passage of all sorts of wheeled objects: wheelbarrows, lawn mowers, baby carriages, wheelchairs and shopping carts. Within the landscape itself, earthen, grassed ramps are useful as well in providing a means for maneuvering garden equipment around steep banks.

NIGHT LIGHTING

Enjoyment of your outdoors need not end with dusk. Night lighting is an art in itself. Subdued lighting can completely transform the landscape and give it a magical quality. The silhouettes, shadows and odd shapes it brings out have a beauty all their own.

Night lighting is functional, aesthetic and a little mysterious. Soft illumination dramatizes landscape features and plant materials. It makes steps and walkways safe and negotiable after dark. Done well, lighting is beautiful to look at from both the terrace and from indoors. Fixtures located beyond the terrace make the garden part of the night environment and, incidentally, draw insects away from seating areas.

The lighting should be soft, diffused and reflected. It is meant to highlight the garden, *not* to floodlight it. Night illumination is not the same as security lighting. Too often people use overly bright, harsh lighting outdoors. The unpleasant result is a blinding contrast of pinpointed bright light against impenetrable blackness.

In illumination, it is the feature being lighted that is important, not the source of the light. Light sources should not be overly apparent in the garden. Place them so that an observer never has to look directly into or walk across a beam of light. Similarly, strong lighting aimed down onto a terrace tends to be unpleasantly surrealistic. The object is not to spotlight your guests like criminals, but to surround them with a soft, glowing landscape. Indirect light is always preferable. If lights are affixed to trees put them above the lower branches. Twenty feet is a good height.

The branches then will hide the fixture, diffuse and soften the light and create interesting shadows.

Light fixtures that are *meant* to be seen, such as lights on terraces and paths, are best positioned below eye-level. These ornamental light fixtures ought to be restrained and use low-intensity bulbs. Bulbs (120 watts) of clear, white light are usually sufficient anywhere in the landscape. Colored filters can be used too. They work particularly well with water features, but otherwise tend to be garish and are usually unnecessary for residences. Use them with care. The exception is the use of yellow light on the terrace to discourage insects.

The final arrangement and placement of the lighting is a matter of trial and error. To get the best results be prepared to test out various patterns at night. This is not a particularly easy task to do well, but it can make for an enjoyable evening. The easiest testing methods are to use either a heavy-duty, portable light fixture with long extension cords or a powerful flashlight. With one person acting as the observer/judge, another can then move through the darkened landscape illuminating various objects for desirable results. Various angles should be tried out. Also if several lights or flashlights are used, you can test the effects of different multiple lighting patterns as well. If you try this you should remember that flashlights send out a beam of light while a portable light will give off a centralized, diffuse form of illumination. Each has its advantages. Flashlights are simple to work with, but portable lights allow you to test various watt bulbs. With a make-shift shade their lighting can be more easily focused and angled.

There is no simple formula for landscape illumination since a change in the number of lights, their location, the direction, intensity and angle of the beam will each dramatically change the effect. You can plan ahead to the extent of *thinking* about what to illuminate, however. Then, having *decided,* you can position and bury the cables during the site's preparation. This at least fixes the outlet locations and avoids the upheaval of burying cables later.

All fittings have to be grounded for safety, and cables, above or below ground, must be weather- and childproof. Submersible fixtures should be used in wet spots and in pools.

Recently low-voltage lighting has become available for garden

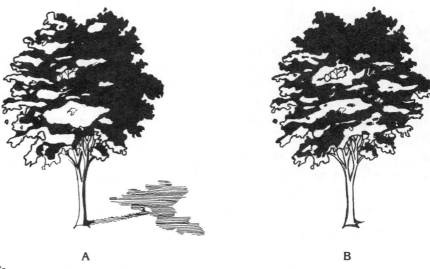

A

B

A tree illuminated from four directions—(A) from the left, (B) up lighting, (C) back lighting, and (D) inside of the tree.

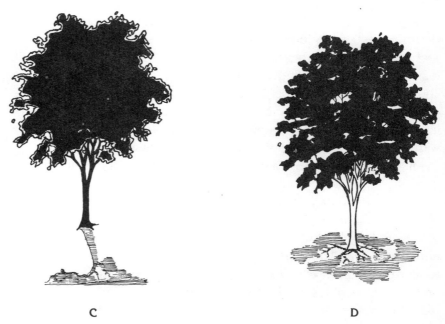

C

D

use. It is extremely safe lighting. The electric charge is so low that it rarely even causes a shock. It is also less expensive to install and maintain. The utility bills are low since it uses so little power and the cables need not be heavily protected and buried. All that is required is a transformer to reduce the typical residential current of 120 volts to 12 volts. Your local electrician will have more details.

One final comment. Use several lights in the landscape. Six softer lights will be much more effective than one or two powerful ones. Homeowners often position a floodlight high up in an effort to do the job that two or three smaller lights near the ground would do far better.

FENCES

Fencing is an important structural landscape element that homeowners often overlook. Fences can provide security, act as windbreaks, buffer noise, offer instant privacy, screen out objectionable views, tie the home to the land, separate activities, and perhaps most important, serve as space definers. Their special beauty is that they can do all these things in an extremely narrow space. No other separating element requires so little room to accomplish these functions.

Space Definers. Fences literally create spaces by partially or totally enclosing them. They can extend interior spaces out into the landscape and expand the architectural impact of your home. Entrances can be clarified and defined with them and "outdoor rooms" can be created within the fencing.

Climatic Modifiers. Fences influence a site's microclimate by blocking winds and snow and by trapping the sun's heat.

Security. The original purpose of fencing was to keep people or animals in or out. This function is still valid, although in residential design today this usually means small children and pets. There is a definite psychological factor involved as well. Even a low fence will act to discourage trespassers and felons.

Screening. An obvious function of fencing is to block out or screen objectionable views on or off the property, to buffer noises and to provide privacy. Within the yard itself they can also hide garbage cans, storage and work areas, exterior utilities or other undesirable spots. One advantage of fencing is that it offers an immediate solution to such problems, while a screen of vegetation may take years to mature.

Among the numerous fencing types available commercially or that you can build yourself, many are attractive. The negative connotations that the word "fence" sometimes evokes—the mental image of a six-foot high wire-mesh security fence—is false. Fencing can be beautiful as well as functional.

Fences do not have to enclose an entire yard or property either. They can be well utilized in short sections as screens or to highlight specific areas. They are excellent for creating partial enclosures, clarifying entrances and circulation, and as a background for planting. An additional bonus of fencing is the shadow-play that is created against them. Subtle, delicate, moving shadows add an interesting element to any garden area.

The appropriate type of fence to choose depends on a number of things: location, function, architectural style of the home, context of the property (urban or rural), the degree of formality desired, and topography. It also depends on whether the fence is primarily utilitarian or decorative in nature.

In general:

1. If neighboring houses are close by, you will need *more* and *higher* fencing in order to insure privacy. Also, the denser the neighborhood structure the more important it is for fencing styles to be coordinated and consistent throughout.

2. On typical suburban lots it is usually best to allow at least partial visual access across close property lines. Otherwise the landscape will be cut up by the fencing. Keep the context of your property—its neighborhood character—in mind when you consider fencing. Since a fence should never be an intrusion in the landscape it is recommended, in suburban situations, that you do not fence in your entire property.

3. Be considerate of your neighbors. Never use a boundary fence with only one good side if you want to remain on friendly terms with them. Try not to box them in or cut off their pleasant views.

4. Fences should blend in with the surroundings. That is one reason natural wood fencing is a perennial favorite. Age weathers it to an attractive, unobtrusive color that more than makes up for

what it lacks in durability compared to metal fencing. (Natural wood fences should be treated with preservatives for increased longevity.) Wood and metal fencing is expensive, but they are relatively maintenance-free once in place compared to a hedge, for example, which requires constant clipping and several years to mature.

5. Fencing is not normally meant to serve as a center of interest in the garden. Its main functions will be as a backdrop to planting and as a space definer. Trees and shrubs can be used to soften up the strong horizontal line of a fence. Indeed, fences and plant material should be used together to make complementary combinations.

6. Fencing should be above *or* below the average eye-level. It should be clear whether it is intended to be seen over or not. Solid fences in the five foot height range should be avoided for this reason if possible.

The architectural style of the home and the relative property size are probably the most important factors affecting the proper choice of fence types. An old-fashioned picket fence is not compatible with a contemporary home and vice versa. The fencing type must relate the dwelling's architectural style. The closer the fence is to be to the home the truer this becomes. Generally, the further from the home, the lower and more transparent the fencing should be.

Transparency and height are the simplest ways of categorizing fencing types. Based on how much light, air movement, and visibility is possible through a fence, they can be characterized as solid, semi-transparent, and open. Since the appropriate height of a fence is usually closely related to its degree of transparency these basic elements will be considered together.

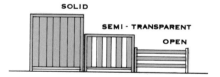

Solid fences are generally best used directly adjacent to or attached to the dwelling itself. A corresponding height of between five to eight feet is recommended since solid fences are usually used for privacy. These fences should be very close in style, color and materials to the home. Semi-transparent fencing, partially open to the eye and the elements, can be less closely related to the home's architecture. They are often finished in natural tones. A three and a half to six foot height is suggested and they are best used adjacent or totally separate from the

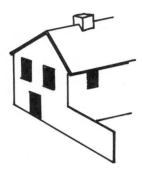

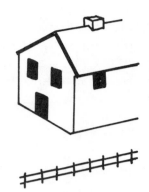

The relationship of solid, transparent and open fencing to a dwelling

Fencing and topography

COMMON FENCE TYPES

1. Panel
2. Basketweave
3. Contemporary Rail
4. Split-rail
5. Wire mesh
6. Stockade
7. Board
8. Picket
9. Louvered

house. Open fences are the opposite of solid. They should be as unobtrusive as possible with minimal visual obstruction. They also should be located away from the dwelling and be relatively low—three to four feet. Split rail and wire and timber fences are examples of open fencing. They are most appropriate in rural settings where privacy is not an issue.

Your property's topography also directly affects the choice of fence types. The more solid the fence, the flatter the site it will require. Semi-transparent fencing is best for gently rolling topography. Steeper slopes are well suited to open fence types since the posts can more easily follow the ground forms. Fortunately this fits the topography of most homes as the land tends to be flattest near the dwelling and becomes more rolling as you move away.

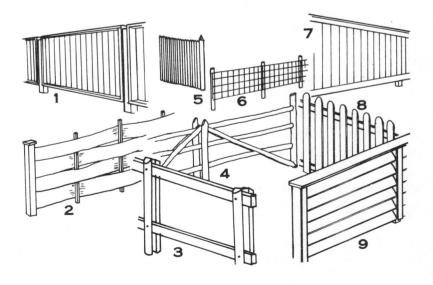

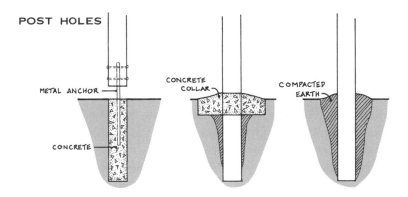

POST HOLES

METAL ANCHOR

CONCRETE COLLAR

COMPACTED EARTH

CONCRETE

Dozens of fence styles are available everywhere in this country. The types and styles most appropriate to your situation are not difficult to find. With all the landscape functions fencing can fulfill, they deserve your consideration.

WALLS

Walls are strong architectural elements that lend a special clarity to landscape schemes. They can fulfill all the functions of fencing and be used to retain earth as well, making one or more level areas possible in the landscape. There is a richness and permanence to walls that cannot be duplicated by a fence or hedge.

Walls are classified as either free-standing—used for enclosure purposes—or as retaining, which, as the name implies, are designed to hold back earth. Free-standing walls are less massive than retaining walls and are used as space definers within the landscape or as boundary markers. Retaining walls are appropriate when a smooth gradient between adjacent level areas is impossible. This is the case when the slope is very severe and/or where spatial limitations rule out the desirability of a long gradual embankment. The question of available space is an important one in considering retaining walls. They are a more formal treatment of the problem than a natural bank, but do require far less room and are easier to maintain. With them more level space is made available for your enjoyment. Stone and concrete are the recommended materials for retaining wall construction.

Many, many types of walls can be constructed out of the building materials we will discuss: brick, stone, and concrete. It should be emphasized too, that while walls are expensive to install, they are maintenance-free and can add an elegance that is difficult to match.

Some general comments:

1. Walls should only be used where they serve a definite, obvious function. They are strong architectural statements that will look ridiculous if their purpose is not obvious to an observer.

2. In most residential situations retaining walls should be used sparingly. While the terraced effect can be very attractive, these walls also tend to emphasize grade changes and interrupt the natural land flow.

3. Usually the simpler the construction of the wall the better it appears. Walls should be solid, simple and honest. Complex construction will mean higher cost, too.

4. The common practice of putting short and dwarfed walls thoughout the garden is to be avoided. Generally, a two foot minimum in height is recommended.

5. Homeowners should not attempt to construct retaining walls over four or five feet high. Anything beyond that becomes very much of an engineering problem.

6. Most walls will require a solid footing for stability. With retaining walls especially, it is necessary to go down below the frost depth for the particular area. This can mean four feet below ground or more in our northern states.

7. Pierced or narrow walls ought to be used within the garden area only, not along the boundary.

8. Retaining walls are of three basic types: gravity, cantilever and counterfort. Only the first should be attempted by novice stonemasons. If a gravity wall is to be built, you must provide for drainage around or through the wall. Gravel can be used behind the wall to ease drainage problems; drainage tiles can be installed and/or weep holes built through the wall.

Weep holes can be made by either using earthenware piping slanting up and through the wall or by leaving out a few vertical jointers out of brick and stone walls. Weep holes should be placed at six foot intervals, six inches above the ground.

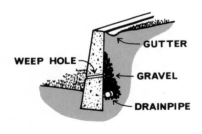

WEEP HOLE

GUTTER

GRAVEL

DRAINPIPE

Brick. Brick is an extremely attractive building material which blends in well with most landscapes. Only in very rustic situations can it appear out of place. Brick walls can be made with numerous variations in the bonding pattern. The exterior brick chosen should be a hard, durable type.

Walls are usually made two bricks thick (9″), except for the Jeffersonian serpentine wall which is of limited application. The double thickness gives the wall mass and stability and alleviates the need for buttressing (side supports) in most cases.

Concrete foundations will often be necessary for stability and in rainy climates a damp-proof course may be needed to protect the brick from decay. Capping the wall (coping) also protects it somewhat from the elements and enhances its appearance. Brick coping, with the individual bricks set on a slant, is the traditional method. Precast concrete and tile copings and cut stone offer attractive alternatives. These latter are very weather-resistant. If possible the coping material should be used elsewhere in the design. For example, a brick wall enclosing a cut stone terrace probably ought to have the same cut stone used as coping for reasons of continuity.

If done with great care, tile, statuary niches, metal grillwork and stone inserts can be incorporated into brick walls as highlights.

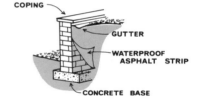

Stone. Nothing can quite compare to a stone wall. In regions where stone is in common use as a building material, it is the ideal choice for a wall. It is usually best to use native stone and to conform to local construction techniques.

The most familiar stone walls are coursed walls—where the stone is layered like brick with the occasional stone taking up two or more courses—and random rubble walls, which are built of irregular, unpatterned stone. If you are building a coursed wall be sure to truly layer the stone so that lines run in a horizontal

Coursed and random rubble walls

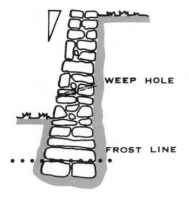

In this stone retaining wall note that the base is twice as wide as the top and how the face of the wall slants into the hill at an angle.

pattern across the wall, not vertically or otherwise. In both random and coursed walls use big stones. Lots of little stones will be easier to move but make for an awkward-looking wall.

If the stone is to be used in a gravity retaining wall, remember that not only must the wall extend below the frostline, but it should be constructed so that the bottom is almost twice as thick as the top. Stone retaining walls can be either mortared or laid dry. If they are dry walls (unmortared), small rock plants can be incorporated into the wall itself. Also remember to include weep holes for drainage! (See general comments.)

Concrete. Concrete walls can be given a wide variety of surface treatments and need not be overly massive or cold in appearance. Both concrete block and poured concrete walls can be used satisfactorily in urban and rural situations. If block is used the color should be picked with care, though, and all types of concrete walls look far better if they are properly capped. Precast concrete coping slabs are a simple, economical solution. Avoid harsh, metallic colors. Remember too that the concrete's surface can be richly textured, troweled, stuccoed, or sand and pebbles brushed into the surface.

Pierced and Veneer Walls. These deserve separate attention. Pierced walls are semi-transparent walls usually built of precast block or brick. These walls make excellent partial screens within the garden area where privacy is not a priority. They have the advantage of allowing some visual connection between different areas while still acting as effective space delineators. The open design pattern within the blocks themselves and the repeating positive and negative rhythms in such walls as a whole can be very attractive. Nevertheless, pierced walls should be used with care. They are best over short distances since their pattern becomes overbearing and monotonous over long stretches. As free-standing walls they are simple to erect and require no reinforcement. Local building supply houses will carry several precast, pierced blocks or you may choose to build with solid block or brick, staggering them to create patterned openings.

Veneer walls offer the rich appearance of traditional walling, but are much less expensive to construct. The secret is in putting an attractive facing on an inexpensive material. Usually lightweight block or hollow tiles are covered by a thin layer brick or

Spaced brick patterns

Precast concrete blocks

stone veneer. This facing need only be inches thick. There are two drawbacks, the first being that the veneer technique is generally limited to free-standing walls, not retaining walls, and should be used only where one face of the wall will be visible. Veneering both sides cancels out cost advantage. The second problem is that the veneer chosen must have the appearance of authenticity. Many commercial veneers are in questionable taste and obviously false-looking. It is best to choose a veneer that is made of the material to be imitated; for example, a brick veneer ought to be thin brick, not a synthetic substitute.

Timber "Walls" and Rip-Rap. Wooden poles and railroad ties are occasionally used in retaining wall construction. Although not true walls in the traditional sense, they can be quite effective. They can also cost less than brick, concrete, or stone. Vertical timber poles can also be used to construct free-standing screens. This is particularly effective if the pole heights are varied.

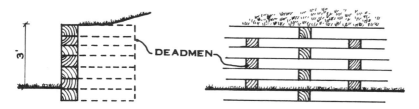

Lastly, since walls are often drastic solutions to embankments, rip-rapping should be mentioned. On slopes of less than 45 degrees where a wall may not be an acceptable solution, other methods of slope stabilization are possible. Aside from binding together the bank's soils with vegetation, rip-rap, a protective surface layer of stone, block, or rarely, wooden poles can be used. This is not a typical rock garden, since the stone or other material will totally dominate any scattered, incidental relief plantings. Used in extreme situations and with care, rip-rap can be a successful solution within the home landscape.

HARD SURFACES

Paving can be the single most important architectural element in the landscape. Both functional and aesthetic factors need to be carefully weighed in laying out paved areas and in choosing the appropriate paving material(s) for your site.

The hard surfacing materials to be covered here include: poured concrete and unit materials such as brick, stone, concrete slabs, tile, wood sections and adobe. How these materials can be dry-laid or mortared into place will be individually discussed. It should be mentioned that while hard paving materials are more expensive than softer surfacing treatments, such as grass or gravel, they are far more practical, wear-resistant, and maintenance-free and allow for better drainage control.

Basically, the purpose of hard surface paving is to provide level, dry, easily walkable outdoor activity areas and to allow for passage to or between such areas and the natural environment. Paving also can define and separate various use areas from one another. For this reason a roadway crosswalk, an entry landing, or a seating area off of a pathway may often have a noticeably different surface treatment. A change in the materials used, its color or texture indicates a change in activities between adjacent spaces. In these examples, they say "caution—walk here" (crosswalk), "you have arrived" (landing) and "sit and relax" (seating area). So, if your paved areas and walkways serve different functions, as they assuredly will, do not hesitate to use different paving materials to emphasize these changes.

Aesthetically, a good landscape design should be planned around your hard surfaced use areas since these areas will normally be the most permanent and heavily used outdoor areas and because they offer both physical and visual access to the rest of your landscape. Designing paved areas is an art in itself. Texture, color, line, and pattern all need to be considered in addition to the proper placement of the hard surface areas themselves within your landscape design.

Outdoor flooring can range in texture from glassy smooth to very coarse and rough. Texture here means both its visual appearance and its tactile qualities—how it feels underfoot. Smooth surfacing allows for quick, easy passage and tends to recede and become unobtrusive. Rougher surfaces call attention to themselves and are harder to negotiate. People tend to look down at rough surfacing, if only to be sure they won't trip!

The color(s) of the paving material(s) is clearly important too. Harsh, metallic, cold colors do not blend in well with the surrounding environment. The surfacing should not be in sharp contrast to the other colors in the house and neighboring landscape. Also whether the paving is light or dark affects the micro-climate around the paved area. Light colors reflect the sun's heat, making a cool, but glaring surface, while dark colors absorb heat for a hotter, non-glaring surface. Of the two, glare is generally acknowledged to be the more pressing of the problems.

In addition to the placement and orientation of the surfaced areas within your design scheme, the lines and patterns in the paving materials themselves can also be used to define boundaries and emphasize direction. In the same way that a terrace's form or a path's location physically lead a person, lines and patterns within the paving material can direct him visually. The use of different materials, choice of bonding patterns or changing the color and/or tecture in the material's surface treatment can be skillfully employed in this way. A simple example of this is shown in the following illustrations. Paving blocks laid perpendicular to an observer convey a feeling of width and foreshortening, while the same blocks laid along his sight line convey depth.

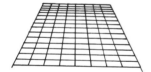 

1. Continuity. It is best if the chosen paving material(s) is repeated, in some form, elsewhere in the landscape or dwelling. This promotes continuity and linkage between the various elements. A brick home, for instance, with a proposed concrete terrace could have brick as an edging to the terrace or perhaps rectangular concrete slabs with brick strips between them. Similarly if a concrete walkway leads to a large patio where a change in the surface treatment might be desirable, concrete should probably remain a component of the patio. This allows the paving to reflect the change in activity without destroying its basic continuity.

DESIGN HINTS FOR PAVING

2. Color. In general, relatively dark surfacing materials are recommended for sunny locations and lighter materials for shade areas.

3. Drainage. Drainage is crucial on paved areas since these areas are relatively flat by nature. Make sure that all drainage is directed away from the house and that all hard surfacing has at least a one or two percent slope to it.

4. Size Allotment. Be generous in allotting space to paved areas. Whether it is a driveway, a walk, or a terrace, something larger than the minimum size will be an asset.

5. Material Availability. Try to use locally available paving materials whenever possible. Not only may materials exotic to your area prove to be out of place, but they will be expensive too.

6. Large Expanses of Paving. In residential situations, large expanses of paving of any one kind are monotonous and should usually be broken up or softened with vegetation, furniture, potted plants, or by varying paving materials or surface treatments.

7. Paving Unit Size. As a general rule, the smaller the paving material's unit size the more suitable it usually is for private gardens; for example, bricks are better than four by four concrete blocks which are better than uninterrupted poured concrete. Conversely, the larger the unit size the more appropriate they normally are for large public spaces.

8. Variations within a Given Building Material. Similarly, the more variety that exists between the individual units of a paving material, the more suited it is for intimate garden situations. The variations in uncut, natural stone are generally more appropriate in such conditions than a uniformly shaped, smooth concrete block.

9. Combinations of Paving Materials. The use of two or even three different materials in a paved area can definitely add richness to your landscape, but it also can be easily overdone. A strong, simple pattern using no more than three paving types is suggested. A paved area that utilizes several materials or has a complex pattern will appear to be smaller and more cluttered than an area of identical size that uses only one or two paving materials in a straightforward pattern. Remember, too, that paving types should not be indiscriminately mixed. Some materials such as brick and concrete are very compatible, but other combinations can be less successful if not handled with care.

COMBINATIONS OF PAVING MATERIALS
a—concrete and brick
b—brick with wood headers
c—asphalt with concrete dividers
d—concrete slabs and cobblestone or gravel.

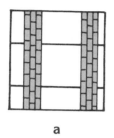
a

b

c

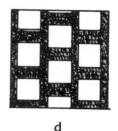
d

10. Modules. Basing the design of your large, outdoor paved areas on a modular unit may save time. Rectangular units are also the simplest to work with. How these units are treated and with what material(s) will depend on your particular situation. (See heading for Terraces, Patios, and Decks.)

11. Curved Paving. If curved paved areas are called for in your design, you may want to reconsider since the cost and difficulty of installation will be far more than for uncurved areas. Poured concrete is the most adaptable material for curves.

Brick. Versatile brick is an attractive material well suited to do-it-yourself paving projects. Unfortunately, it is not an inexpensive material, but its many attributes will often outweigh the cost factor. Brick is: readily available in a wide range of colors from dark red to light yellow, relatively easy to install, excellent in combination with other paving materials, and can be laid in innumerable patterns. The small size of the individual building units has advantages, too. The size allows brick paved areas to accommodate gradual slopes and is adaptable to curved and

HARD PAVING CONSTRUCTION MATERIALS

irregular forms. Since individual bricks can be cut, brick is particularly suited for odd shapes and sharp corners. In addition, the numerous possible brick paving patterns can be laid so as to bring out design lines. These lines can be used to lead the eye and repeat other lines in the landscape. (See Line under Principles and Elements of Design.)

BRICK PAVING PATTERNS

herringbone

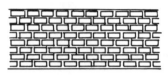

running band

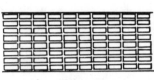

jack-on-jack

basketweave

herringbone at 90°

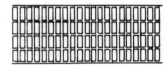

soldiers

Bricks can be laid dry or mortared. Either way a hard, durable exterior brick type is recommended for outdoor paving and some sort of subsurface base will usually be needed. The type of base required depends on drainage, depth of frost and the anticipated use of the paved area. The poorer the drainage, the more severe the winters, and the heavier the anticipated use, the deeper and more permanent the base will need to be.

Dry-laid bricks are laid on a sand base six to twelve inches deep depending on the factors listed above. Bricks on sand are best laid with closed joints, separations of no more than one-quarter inch between the bricks. After the bricks are down, dry sand or a mixture of one part cement, three parts fine sand should be brushed in between the cracks and wetted down. For a more stable, permanent area, the brick should be mortared on top of a concrete sub-base.

DRY-LAID

— cement & sand mixture brushed into joints dry & wetted

— 2" sand

— 2" compacted gravel

MORTARED

— 3/4" mortar bed

— 4" concrete slab

— 4" compacted gravel

Adobe is a close cousin to brick and can be treated and laid in similar ways. Like brick its natural color and low maintenance requirement make it ideal for home use. Moreover, adobe is now often strengthened with asphalt stabilizers to be stronger and longer lasting than old-fashioned adobe. Inexpensive and widely available in the Southwest, adobe is unfortunately not a common or cheap building material elsewhere. Only if an adobe manufacturer is nearby should this material be considered by home-owners.

Concrete. Concrete is an excellent paving material. Less expensive than brick or stone, concrete can be very attractive. It does not have to be dull and gray. As with concrete walls, the surface can be treated several ways—brushed, troweled, color added to the wet mix and various aggregates sprinkled on or in the mix. In fact, if a large, concrete paved area is proposed for a garden setting, some surface treatment will probably be necessary to soften the material. Concrete is also excellent in combination with other paving materials, particularly brick and wood. Used as insert patterns, edging or dividers, these other materials can pleasantly break up large expanses of concrete.

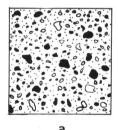

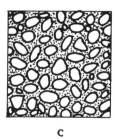

a   b   c

TEXTURES:
a—aggregate
b—troweled
c—cobble set in wet concrete

Concrete can be poured in place or bought as precast slabs. If it is to be poured in place, remember to "score" the surface every six to eight feet. Scores allow for temperature shrinkage and prevent cracking by incorporating weak points at specific intervals within the surface. Poured concrete is one of the least expensive paving materials available. It can be overbearing in many domestic situations, however, if the surface is not treated or if the expanse is not broken down into smaller units.

A typical mix is: one part cement, two parts sand, and three parts aggregate (gravel). If you are doing the work yourself read

Score line

Wooden divider

and follow mixing and laying directions closely. Watch the temperature too. Do not lay concrete in cold weather when a freeze is possible or in very hot temperatures (+90°).

Concrete Slabs. Precast concrete slabs of various sizes are widely available to homeowners today and deserve consideration, since they are relatively inexpensive and easy to handle and install. These slabs come in several colors, shapes and surface treatments and are usually one and a half to two inches thick. Their many available shapes and sizes allow you to create different patterns with them. Since they are independent building units no scoring is necessary. As with bricks the slabs can be dry laid on a sand sub-base or laid and mortared on concrete. Durable, versatile, and cheap, concrete precast slabs are fast becoming the most common residential paving material.

Stone. Unequalled as a paving material, stone's natural beauty only mellows with age. It is particularly suited to rural and older urban situations. Stone is costly, however, especially if it is cut or hauled long distances. Cut stone has a formal, polished appearance and its regular shapes make it easier to install and form patterns with. Uncut, irregular stone is more naturalistic and informal. Since the individual stones' shapes and thicknesses vary, it can be fairly difficult to work with. Stone is also an obviously heavy building medium, but try to avoid using small stones in place of heavier large ones. The result is nearly always unsatisfactory.

With cut stone—such as slate, granite, or greenstone—it will help if you work out the basic paving pattern before you order the stone. The pattern will give you a better handle on the quantity and shape of stones needed.

The pleasant, random appearance of irregular stone paving is hard to surpass. If you have access to local fieldstone, this type of paving can be had fairly cheaply, though the work is backbreaking. Such informal paved areas can be enhanced if the edging is not too hard, but flows somewhat loosely into the surroundings. It should also be remembered that irregular stones are not easy to walk on and every effort needs to be made to make the paved area as level as possible.

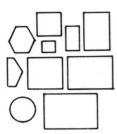

Concrete slabs come in many sizes and shapes.

Stone of any kind can be laid in sand, concrete, or in soil. While the latter is the simplest, it is often unsatisfactory since the stones will heave up in cold winters. The procedure for sand and concrete sub-bases are the same as those for brick or concrete slabs.

LESS COMMON HARD PAVING MATERIALS

Cobbles. Cobbles are large rounded pebbles from one to ten inches in diameter. They make an extremely rough paving, but one that is useful in selected locations as a relief feature within paved areas and for otherwise awkward spaces. Generally, cobbles are best set into wet concrete by hand and packed very close together. The rich texture and variety cobble can give to a paved area is outstanding, but it is hard to walk on.

Precast Tiles. Precast tiles are similar to concrete slabs in terms of their ready availability and wide variety of colors and textures. They are expensive, but not too difficult to install. A concrete sub-base is necessary for tile surfacing. Like cobble, tiles can be an excellent accent or relief feature with other paving materials and, used in the right situations, can be very attractive.

Sawn Log Sections. Sawn log sections can also be set into concrete with positive results. The sections should be treated with wood preservatives to prevent rot and be at least an inch and a half thick. If a hard, treated wood is used you will have many years of service from such a surface. Clean sawn, round, grained log sections create an interesting pattern all their own and one that blends in well with informal surroundings.

Gravel. Gravel is not a true hard surfacing material since it makes a loose surface, but a word needs be said for it here. Loose gravel is in its own way an excellent surfacing. Relatively cheap and durable—if not subject to heavy or intensive use—gravel is particularly suited for covering large areas that might appear oppressive if surfaced in a hard material like concrete or asphalt. For that reason one occasionally sees gravel used on broad paths and entry drives. It can be purchased in several gauges (sizes) and various colors—greys, browns and creams being the most common. Gravel is not easy to walk on, however, expecially when wet, and periodically will need to be replenished to cover settled areas and inhibit weed growth. Washed pea gravel is recommended and local availability is a crucial cost factor. For garden use a sub-base of large, course gravel three inches thick needs to be laid first, followed by two separate laid two inch layers of fine pea gravel. Each layer will need to be rolled for stability as it is placed.

In choosing paving materials keep in mind the context of the area to be paved. Its appropriateness to the site needs to be well considered. Also don't be too easily swayed by your preferences or the cost differences between various materials. Function has to be the primary consideration in choosing a paving material. One additional cost factor does have to be considered, however. Paving, especially intricate, complicated paving surfaces, is difficult work. Laborers skilled enough for the work can sometimes be hard to find and they will be expensive when found. Remember to weigh installation costs as well.

NOTE: Only the major landscape elements have been covered in this chapter. The many minor, special elements are far too numerous to try to cover adequately in one book. For information on such features as outdoor furniture, sculpture, swimming and garden pools, outbuildings, fountains, greenhouses, raised planters, and so forth, it is better to go to publications specializing in them. (See Bibliography.)

CHAPTER 11

Mobile and Modular Homes and Condominiums

The "mobile" in mobile homes is somewhat of a misnomer since few are actually moved after their initial trip from the factory. Ninety percent reportedly never move. Mobile homes are here to stay and their rapidly growing number of owners deserve special attention. Indeed, mobile homes may need landscaping more than any other form of detached housing. With a price range of between $12,000-$40,000, they are affordable, residential structures and are becoming increasingly competitive with more expensive, traditional houses. Aesthetically, mobile homes have been a disaster in the past, but new designs and proper landscaping can go a long way towards improving their livability and appearance.

The Design Process outlined in the text is as valid for mobile homes as for any other type of housing. Nevertheless, three additional factors need to be given special consideration: the shape of the unit, its landscape context and anchoring.

An elongated, rectangular, box-like form is the underlying shape of the vast majority of mobile homes. Even in double-wide units which may include a peaked roof, this basic form dominates. Located on a site this rectangular shape will tend to stand out in stark contrast to its surroundings. This conveys an image of transient impermanence. The home does not belong to the land since it does not appear to relate to it in any way. Factory delivered units do not include any transition zones that would blend it in more gradually with the landscape. The exterior materials, colors and the shape in general all reinforce a total separation between the mobile homes and the land. Being a

MOBILE HOMES

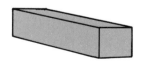

foundationless structure only compounds the problem. As a result, the mobile home is not anchored or tied down to the site either physically or visually.

Landscaping can solve these particular problems in addition to creating more usable and attractive spaces around the mobile home unit. Obviously, the use of skirts and plantings to hide the hitches, tanks, and underspace is the first step. Secondly, architectural features should be added to soften the rectangular shape, create transition zones between the unit and the landscape and anchor it firmly to the site. Fencing, porches, decks, carports, attached garages, raised planters, trellis work, awnings, lighting fixtures, sidewalks, patios, and plantings in general can all fulfill these functions. Which you choose will depend on your particular needs and budget and on the site itself.

There is no reason in the world why these features cannot be added to mobile home units. With a little imagination and judicious landscaping a modern mobile home can be made an attractive, functional dwelling.

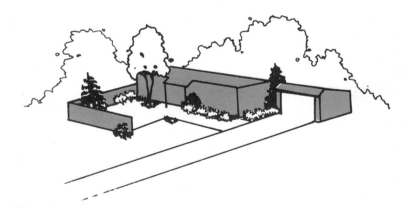

There are, unfortunately, circumstances that often discourage owners of mobile homes from making permanent landscape improvements—one is the situation of being a lessee in a trailer park, the other is the issue of property taxation. This tax rate is often directly tied to the apparent mobility of the home itself. This is counterproductive since the first step in mobile home landscaping is to treat the unit and its surroundings as a residential structure, lessening the appearance of its mobility. Check the local ordinances and tax classifications before you do your designing. Remember though that many of these suggested architectural elements can be movable themselves, such as shrubs in planters instead of in the ground, patios dry-laid rather than mortared. Fencing, trellises, awnings, even lighting fixtures can be installed in such a manner that they can be taken with you if you do choose to move your unit.

Mobile Home Parks. A word needs to be said on mobile home parks as well. These parks can be extremely well done. A well planned and laid out mobile home park can convey an impression very similar to a neighborhood subdivision. They are sometimes laid out with the major landscape work already completed and may include well maintained common spaces and community amenities such as playground and recreational facilities. If you are looking into parks, be sure to consider the landscaping of the park in general and of the individual pads. Often the individual landscaping of each pad will be required of the lessee. Careful planning will be necessary as these pads are usually quite small in size.

MODULAR HOUSING

This type of housing is also becoming increasingly prevalent, but it is available in so many forms and styles that it is far more difficult to treat as a distinct case. There is, for instance, no sterotypical modular housing. In general, they are now designed and constructed as well as most conventional housing. Shape, a particular issue in mobile homes, does not apply since the modules can be arranged in numerous, varied arrangements. Modular housing, then, is best treated as one would approach any typical dwelling, that is by following the Design Process. If the housing is high density—close together—you may want to read the following section on cluster housing.

CLUSTER HOUSING

Cluster housing refers to high-density housing types, with particular emphasis on townhouses, garden apartments, and condominiums.

These types of housing tend to have small, close private lots

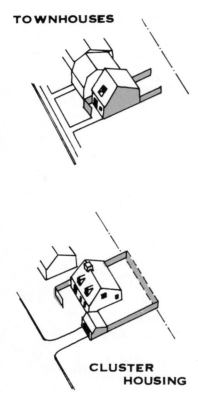

TOWNHOUSES

CLUSTER HOUSING

that require the extensive use of fencing, walls, plant materials, and terraces or patios for both enclosure (privacy) purposes and to maximize the usefulness of the limited outdoor space. Under these conditions fencing should be at least five feet, or preferably, six feet high, to insure privacy. Major plant materials will tend to be more supportive of the architectural elements than is usually the case in detached single family homes. They will serve to complement, extend and soften the harder architectural elements.

Also, with space at a premium, a functional outdoor, hardsurfaced area is essential. Ideally, this area should be planned to allow for relief plantings, a small garden, and outdoor furniture. Treating your limited outdoor space as a courtyard usually has satisfactory results. The paving material(s) used may well be the most important single element in your small landscape, so handle the ground plane with care. (See section on Hard Surfaces.) In such spaces interesting low-maintenance ground covers are far superior to odd, minute grassed areas.

The rules and regulations regarding what is allowable in the way of a unit owner's private landscaping initiatives of course varies considerably between different developments. Ideally, common elements such as fencing and lighting that are repeated throughout a development should be controlled for unity and consistency. Likewise, the placement and types of major plant materials that owners may choose to use should also be limited to specific areas and general plant types. While you may feel hampered by these regulations, they are important in avoiding the chaos that would result if total design freedom existed between adjacent units.

Occasionally, too, any proposed landscape work may have to be approved by an established community or homeowner association design review board. Check to see what procedures and/or regulations exist in your community. If no regulations exist, it is strongly urged that you support their adoption.

Usually in such developments all of the major landscape work is completed before the individual units are sold. This and any existing restrictions may leave you with only a limited private, outdoor space and perhaps a public entry area to work with. Nevertheless, these areas are your own to develop and indi-

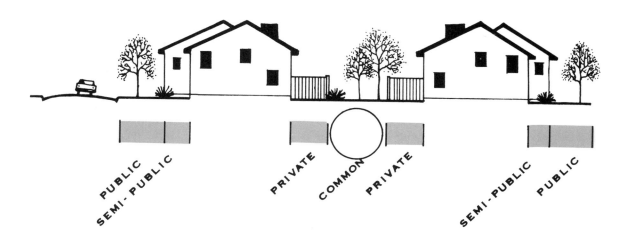

PUBLIC SEMI-PUBLIC PRIVATE COMMON PRIVATE SEMI-PUBLIC PUBLIC

vidualize and the rules, principles and elements outlined in the text still apply. Remember that thorough planning is even more important in areas of limited available space.

The closeness of neighbors means that careful attention has to be given to privacy. The units need to be visually separated and clearly recognizable as individual residences. So think hard about your entrance deck and fencing.

CHAPTER 12

Plants, Trees and Shrubs

COMPOSITION

Being able to artfully arrange plant materials is as important to your landscape as choosing suitable species. Composition is the art of grouping them so that their colors, forms, and textures blend pleasantly together. So far, you have used the basic design principles to locate plant materials to fulfill specific functions and have indicated their general types: deciduous, coniferous, trees, shrubs and groundcovers. Now we must be concerned with their *arrangements* and *interrelationships.* Once the function, location, and grouping of a design's vegetation is determined, it is a simple task to go on to choose and compose the appropriate species.

Since scale and location have been covered elsewhere, we will concentrate here on the problems of form, texture, color, and grouping.

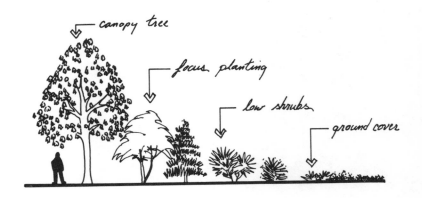

Form. All plant materials have an underlying form or shape. Juxtaposing these shapes in different ways will produce varied results. The above sketch illustrates some of these fundamental vegetation forms. The careful use of different forms can make a planting design much more effective.

Plant forms, especially as exhibited in certain species, often carry strong subconscious associations. They can elicit emotional responses. Wisteria may convey a feeling of nostalgia to you, a weeping willow a sense of melancholy. Above that, basic forms also impart broader impressions. Horizontal forms like juniper shrubs and dogwood give a feeling of width, breadth, and stability. Vertical shapes obviously emphasize height and grandeur.

Texture. Texture is important, too, since it implies weight. A species' branching habit and type of foliage create its texture. Sometimes texture is merely defined as coarse, medium, or fine. A glance out the window will convince you that there is more to it than that. Vegetation can appear as light and open, heavy and tight, rough or smooth, stiff or flexible, and dull or glossy. Using plant materials that have varying textural characteristics adds a subtle richness and elegance to the landscape.

Usually large leaved plants will appear coarser; small leaved ones more delicate. Interestingly, large leaves will also appear to be closer to you, and small leaves further away. Generally, large, open schemes call for coarser plant material and small, compact ones for more delicate textures.

In group plantings or masses, the finer textured plants belong in the front with medium or coarse vegetation behind them to act as a background.

Combining different shapes

Color. Color is obviously important to plant design too. It is also an *extremely* difficult topic to approach. For one thing, there are so many "types" of color in the landscape. Blooms,

Textures: fine, medium, coarse

foliage and bark come in a huge spectrum of colors and are all subject to seasonal changes. Moreover, color preferences are an intensely personal matter. Because the topic is so complex, it seems best to approach it in very broad terms.

Color is a source of constant delight to the observer. As wonderful as it is, it is often, to my mind, overdone. People seem to forget that color exists everywhere in the landscape—even without a bloom in sight. They tend to ignore the wide variety of foliage colors in favor of flowering trees and shrubs. Foliage comes not only in all the shades of green, but in silver-grays, yellows, deep reds and dark purples. In addition there are the seasonal changes in foliage—from the light green of spring, through the deep greens of summer and on to the warm fires of autumn. Particularly if you live in the colder sections of the country these fall colors must be considered in your planning. A planting plan that relies on foliage for color has the advantage of offering long lasting garden colors, as opposed to short-lived blooms. The Japanese have always understood this and their all-green gardens are justifiably famous for subtle beauty.

This is not to downgrade the richness of flowering plants. There is nothing quite so brilliant and beautiful as garden blooms. A word of warning, though. Too many rich contrasting colors can overwhelm a garden quickly. When choosing flowering shrubs, bulbs, and so on, be aware of the *sequence* of colors. Will multi-colored blooms burst out all at once, clashing with each other for attention and then fade, leaving your garden barren again until the following spring? Ideally you should have a series of blooming seasons so that the garden has a touch of color throughout the seasons. With the help of numerous plant books and nursery catalogs this is not difficult to achieve.

The juxtaposition of different colors is very important as well. Bright contrasting colors next to each other will tend to clash. One reason for this is that our eye tends to mix adjacent colors. Two pleasant colors may take on a whole different appearance when placed next to one another. For this reason it is usually best to stay with complementary colors whenever possible.

The point is that color is a very strong element in the landscape and should be treated carefully. It can not only add interest and beauty to the garden but can strengthen your underlying design considerably. Poorly used, it can easily destroy it as well.

Great care is needed especially in the use of strong colors. Variegated foliage and exotic colors should be used sparingly. Most of all be aware of the color relationships you are creating with plant placement.

PLANTING GROUPS AND MASSES

With an understanding of the role that texture, color, and form play in good composition, you can arrange plant materials much more effectively. An excellent way to utilize plant material is to arrange them harmoniously in either groupings or masses. This is much more effective than scattering individual trees, flower beds, shrubs or whatever singly about the yard. Isolated plant materials tend to clutter up a site, negate their use as spatial tools, and cause maintenance problems.

The placement of the plant materials is usually informal. It is nearly always better to group plants than to put them in evenly spaced straight lines.

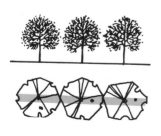 

The triangular arrangement is more interesting and forms a planting group.

In groups or masses, the smaller and/or more finely textured plants belong in the foreground. No more than three or four plant types should be used together and they should normally share some common characteristics in their color, form, or texture. Often too, one plant type should clearly dominate the group with the others being only supportive. Looking at natural plant associations and vegetation clumps will give you useful clues.

 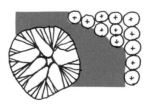

Two plant massings. The left one is a chaos of specie types and shapes while the right example correctly shows simplicity and specie dominance.

TYPICAL PLANTING PROBLEMS

1. Overplanting in *Numbers* and *Types* of Plant Materials. Homeowners tend to go overboard with superfluous plant materials. Using too many different types of vegetation creates a confusing landscape. Overplanting in numbers ignores the size the plants will attain at maturity. The result is cluttered, competing plant materials whose original design intent is lost in a jungle of growth.

2. Demanding an Immediate Effect. Plants take time! Don't be disappointed if your plantings look a little puny at first. To get fast results homeowners too often choose fastgrowing, less desirable species. In certain situations this is quite correct, but if the whole planting plan depends on "quickies," think again. These fast growers are usually softwooded and susceptible to both insect and storm damage. Their useful life-span is often only a few years. It is primarily the slower, but more permanent varieties, that are of lasting value.

3. Forcing Plants. Not matching your particular site's characteristics with a chosen plant's natural habitat is a common mistake. The result will be unhealthy, stunted growth and a high maintenance requirement. Why bother? It is usually better for all but the most dedicated gardeners to stick with species that are tried and proven in your area and whose requirements in terms of soil, sunlight, and moisture can be met in your landscape. A magnolia in New England or a Douglas fir in Georgia is simply out of place. Stick with indigenous plant materials. This is particularly true on informal, wooded sites, where the new introduced species must blend in with the native vegetation for the scheme to succeed.

What is true of the site in general is also valid for specific areas of the property. A sun and water loving shrub planted under the wide, shaded eaves of a house will languish and die. Even a plant native to your region has to have its individual needs for moisture, soil type and sunlight catered to and these conditions vary over your site. So try to match the plants' optimum growing medium with not only the general characteristics of your site, but with the specific conditions within it as well.

4. Poor Placement of Plants and Trees. Planting too close to septic systems, water pipes and wells can quickly cause costly damage. All vegetation thrives on water and will seek it out with an unsuspected strength and tenacity. Maples and willows are notorious for this. Planting too close to foundation walls and ignoring overhead wires is equally foolish. Leave at least ten feet between the foundation wall and any potentially large trees. A medium sized tree can be planted as close as six feet. A sapling today will eventually grow into a giant that can cause heavy structural damage to your house. Don't plant large trees and shrubs under wires either. Not only can storm breakage result in severed wires, but utility companies often can legally remove trees that threaten wiring. Major trees tend to look their best when they are grouped together informally to imitate natural stands. A distance of twelve to fifteen feet between trees is recommended in such grouping for healthy growth.

Placement problems are usually the result of poor location choices, inadequate growth space, or overlooking a particular plant's individual characteristics as they relate to location. The first can be avoided if every plant is located to perform an understood function. Not allowing adequate space for a plant's growth is also a common mistake. Be sure to leave enough room between plants or between a given plant and other landscape elements to allow for its mature size and growth habits. Planting a thorned shrub adjacent to a path or putting a fruit tree over the parking area are examples of overlooking the individual characteristics of plant types. Look for potential conflicts between the plant's characteristics and adjacent activities or plantings.

5. Overuse of Evergreens. A good planting plan includes a mixture of decidous and evergreen plants. Evergreens become too rich and overpowering if they are overused. They will quickly dominate your landscape and can form a dense, dark forest eventually. Aside from that they are expensive and many are finicky about soil conditions. Be sure you use them in combination with deciduous trees and shrubs.

6. Garish Color Combinations. This often happens in unplanned landscapes. Think ahead in terms of color, sequence, and juxtaposition.

7. Timid Plant Compositions. Amateurs seem to have a tendency toward miniature, detailed plantings. To be effective on anything but the smallest sites, plants must be arranged boldly. Remember that the grand scale of the out-of-doors will render timid, small compositions purposeless.

MAKING A PRELIMINARY PLANTING PLAN

Since you now have an idea of the location, function, type (size, deciduous, evergreen, etc.) and composition of the plant materials to be used, you can now organize the information into a preliminary planting plan. Whether this information is included in your final design or developed further into a completed planting plan depends entirely on you. Many homeowners may feel a preliminary plan is as far as they wish to go on their own, others will want to complete a final planting plan. Either way will clarify the number of plants and plant types involved and offer a basis for estimating costs. Be sure to include any existing vegetation that will remain as well as all the proposed plant materials. Showing both gives a much clearer idea of the effects of your design. It will also help in determining proper spacing for the plants.

Once you have located the plant materials on a drawing, there are two different approaches you can take. On the one hand you can designate all the vegetation on the plan by the characteristics you wish it to have. Be as explicit as possible. For example, you should know by now that such and such a plant is meant to be deciduous, four to six feet tall, flowering, shade-tolerant, rounded, and so on. Use as many adjectives as necessary to describe the plant you have envisioned. Or you can fully identify each plant to be used by name. Probably you will fall somewhere in between. Very likely you have already been able to decide in a few cases the particular species called for. Fine. Now the remaining unspecified plants must be selected. Even they may have been narrowed down to a few choices.

At this point you may throw up your hands and take your plan with its plant descriptions to a landscape architect or a nursery. The experts can then fill in the gaps and probably comment on your overall design as well. Or you can decide to proceed plant by plant. With all the knowledge you have about a particular plant's desired characteristics, this is not too difficult. It is merely a matter of finding its name. You already know the characteris-

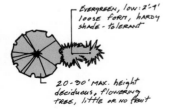

Evergreen, low: 2'-4'
loose form, hardy
shade - tolerant

20-30' max. height
deciduous, flowering
tree, little or no fruit

A preliminary plan is shown below. For additional help in preparing a fully specified planting plan, turn to Project 8 of the Exercises on page 150.

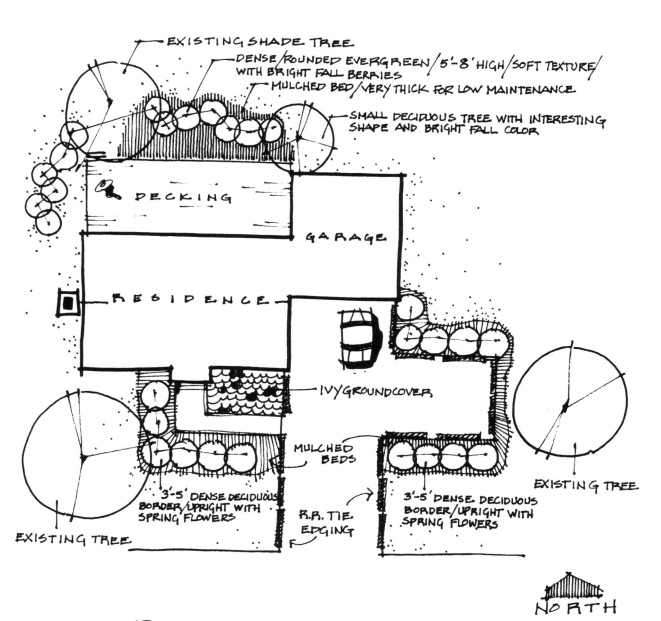

EXISTING SHADE TREE
DENSE/ROUNDED EVERGREEN/5'-8' HIGH/SOFT TEXTURE/ WITH BRIGHT FALL BERRIES
MULCHED BED/VERY THICK FOR LOW MAINTENANCE.
SMALL DECIDUOUS TREE WITH INTERESTING SHAPE AND BRIGHT FALL COLOR

DECKING

GARAGE

RESIDENCE

IVY GROUNDCOVER

MULCHED BEDS

3'-5' DENSE DECIDUOUS BORDER/UPRIGHT WITH SPRING FLOWERS

R.R. TIE EDGING

3'-5' DENSE DECIDUOUS BORDER/UPRIGHT WITH SPRING FLOWERS

EXISTING TREE

EXISTING TREE

NORTH

PLANTING PLAN

tics of both the site and the mystery plant. Matching them to a species can even be fun.

It really is a simple task. There are dozens of books on plant varieties which break down plants by the same characteristics as you have developed. (See Bibliography for plant books.) The local library and garden clubs are good sources, too, since they will carry publications geared to your part of the country. Also nurseries often have lists and catalogs of locally available plants complete with descriptions and prices. As a customer service, a well run nursery will usually be glad to go over your plant choices with you when you visit on plant hunts. Being inquisitive about plants helps too. Solicit the nurseryman's advice and help. Horticulture is a fascinating subject. The reason amateurs have trouble choosing plants is because they are unprepared. They do not know what they need or want. You, on the other hand, have a fairly detailed idea of what you want. Having this information makes selecting the appropriate species easy.

As you narrow down prospective candidates, it normally happens that two or three species will do equally well. When this happens, just take the process a little further. Local availability and price per plant may be the deciding factors, or just your preference for a particular plant type. At this point personal taste can be the final judge without jeopardizing the design.

A word of caution, be sure that you do match the plant to the site! The Big Four in plant selection are: form (shape), size (mature), hardiness (to local weather conditions, pests and diseases), and the plant's desired growing conditions (pH level, type of soil, moisture requirements, sun versus shade, etc.). Other considerations include: life expectancy, growth rate, availability, price, seasonal interest, and maintenance requirements.

Remember, too, that a planting plan can be implemented in phases just like the rest of your design scheme—the foundation plantings in the spring, the boundary shrubs in the fall and so on.

Lastly, when depicting plants on your scheme, the number of plants needed to accomplish some tasks (such as filling the planting bed or creating a hedge) will depend on the recommended spacing between these individual plants. This necessary distance varies considerably between plant types and it is best to consult a nurseryman to establish it. Since you know the area or distance to be covered he will be able to provide this information quickly based on the characteristics of the chosen specie.

CHAPTER 13

Step 7/Completing the Design

With the overall scheme in hand, you have now gone over the specific elements and activity areas. Planning produced the pieces of the puzzle, the overall scheme gave you the puzzle's final shape, and "Getting Down to Specifics" has allowed you to put the two together while always reexamining and refining as the design progressed.

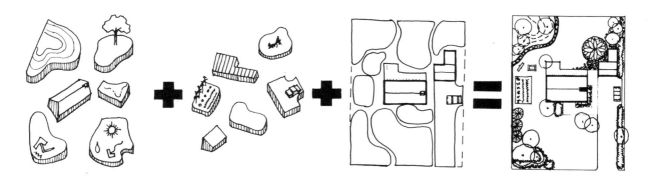

Professionals use the same procedure you have followed because it is logical and comprehensive. Ideally, your finished design should have the amount of detail shown on page 106. For nine out of ten residences, a drawing as basically simple as this is adequate. And don't be concerned if your graphics lack artistic polish. They are fine as long as they are legible to contractors, nurserymen, and most of all, to you.

However, because your finished 17" x 22" drawing will be so much larger than the following illustration it will be able to show

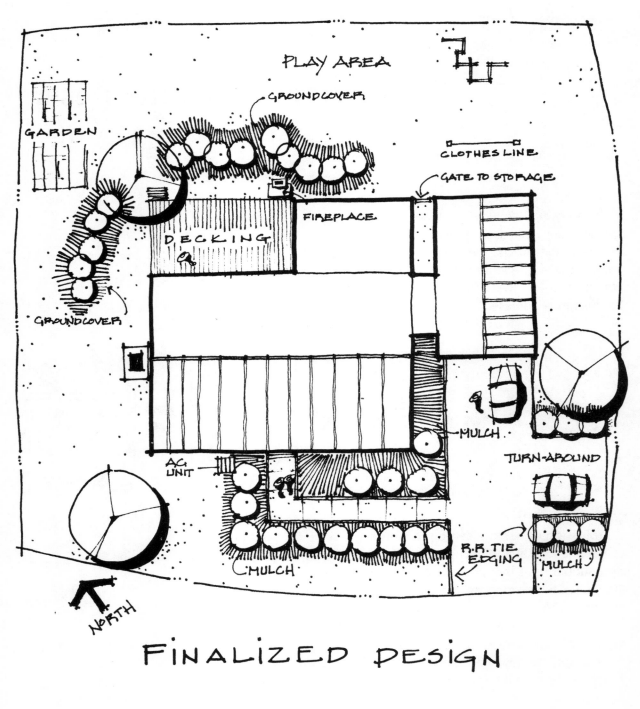

PLAY AREA

GROUNDCOVER

GARDEN

CLOTHES LINE

GATE TO STORAGE

FIREPLACE

DECKING

GROUNDCOVER

MULCH

TURN-AROUND

A.C. UNIT

MULCH

R.R. TIE EDGING

MULCH

NORTH

FINALIZED DESIGN

much more detail. Be sure to label landscape features and note specifications where necessary. Also the finished drawing, if done on graph paper to scale, will show approximate dimensions as well. A contractor or nurseryman should be furnished with all the information they may need on this finished plan.

Since you have followed the step-by-step process, completing the landscape design is relatively simple. The overall scheme must be taken one final step. That step is refining the scheme to decide on the individual details, i.e. the size, materials, and colors of construction and the characteristics of or selected choice of indicated plant material.

Be as thorough as you can. For additional help in translating the landscape scheme into a final design review Chapters 10 and 11 and refer to project 7 in the Exercises.

Creating a landscape design has been greatly simplified by following the 7-step process. You have been able to produce a useful, thorough design and can now proceed with its implementation. While it is hoped that the design experience gave you a sense of accomplishment and was an enjoyable, stimulating task, the lasting pleasure comes now with seeing the scheme become reality and living in and with your own created environment.

The following two sections will deal with implementing your final design and maintaining it in the future.

PART II

CONSTRUCTION
AND MAINTENANCE

CHAPTER 14

Site Preparation, Job Supervision and Staging

The finished drawing(s) now becomes the guide for controlling the design's construction and installation. They insure that the scheme will be carried out as you envisioned it. Cost estimates can be made from the drawing(s), too, and contractors will be able to use them in submitting bids on all or portions of the work to be done. These estimates and bids should be put together early so that budgeting can be worked out satisfactorily.

BUDGET CONSIDERATIONS

Throughout the design process budget considerations were purposely underplayed on the premise that cost-consciousness cramps design freedom. Now the obvious relationships between what you want, what you are willing to pay for it, and what you can afford should be evaluated. If the costs are too high you can pare away less important design components without destroying the plan's integrity. Going the complete route with your design is usually far better, though. If this means staging the plan's installation over several months or years, fine. These stages can be based on your own priorities as long as you keep the necessary sequence of work in mind. For instance, it would not be normally sensible in terms of site disturbance and cost to spread major grading over a long period of time.

An additional factor to consider, beyond the installation costs themselves, is long-term maintenance expenses. Cheap materials and shoddy construction are usually costly to maintain. The opposite is equally true. Quality construction and materials tend to pay for themselves over time by reducing maintenance and saving you time, money and aggravation.

Implementing your final design involves planning ahead. The work's logical sequence must be clearly understood for the design's execution to be properly staged. A mistake here can cause large losses in time and money and endless amounts of frustration.

First, the site must be prepared to receive the design. All the preliminary, subsurface grading work and the installation of any underground wiring or piping should be done at the beginning. Whether you are building a home or merely putting in a new walkway, be sure the initial work is completed before going on.

WHO WILL DO THE WORK?

There are three basic alternatives in delegating the work to be done. The entire job can be given over to a general landscape contractor. This is the simplest, but most expensive, route. Or you yourself can assume the role of the general contractor, either subcontracting out the difficult, specialized tasks or hiring labor as needed. This option requires considerable time on your part, but does give a degree of control over the installation. The third alternative is for you and your family and friends to undertake the entire job yourselves. This offers the least strain on your budget, but the most on your time and energy. Only you can determine if you can afford the time and energy required and are capable of doing the job well yourself.

Many of you will probably farm out the heavier, more complex jobs to local contractors and do the balance of the work yourselves. To get good results you will have to assume the role of the supervisor or job-captain. Supervising the work so that everything is done in order can get complicated. With an extensive plan involving more than one outside contractor, it is helpful to set up a job schedule. This allows each stage to be planned for chronologically. A schedule is useful even if your landscape improvements amount to a series of do-it-yourself weekend projects. It will avoid the annoyance of helpers who don't know what to do next, idle pay-by-the-hour rental equipment, and impatient drivers with truckloads of wet cement. Unanticipated problems and delays will inevitably occur in construction, but a work schedule can eliminate a good many of them.

THE HOMEOWNER AS JOB-CAPTAIN

As the job-captain, it is your task to see that the drawings are followed as closely as possible and to make any adjustments that may be called for. Be attentive to any discrepancies or inaccuracies in the drawings and to their too liberal interpretation by the contractors. Some excellent local contractors are unable to read drawings and it may become necessary to verbally explain their intent to them. Be flexible. During construction, opportunities may arise for improving upon your design and unforeseen problems can force minor changes. You must be prepared to handle these adjustments to your design as quickly as possible.

Even on large-scale projects requiring earthmovers, an informed homeowner can lessen the damage done by overzealous machine operators. These men are experts at handling their equipment, but are notoriously lacking in sensitivity towards the land. They seem to have an uncontrolled urge to level and flatten everything in sight. That may be necessary for a commercial parking lot, but it is not advisable in residential design.

The movement of heavy equipment should be restricted as much as possible on your site. Permit them to go only where it is necessary. They badly maul the landscape. Any trees or shrubs that are to be kept have to be protected from the upheaval that accompanies site preparation. They should be fenced off from the activity. Ideally, no equipment should be allowed closer than the drip-line of major trees (See figure on p. 133). This is because heavy equipment compacts the soil and can literally crush and smother root systems. At the very least, tell the contractors what vegetation is to be saved and mark them in some manner.

DEALING WITH CONTRACTORS

The disparaging remarks towards contractors are meant only as a warning. Most contractors are honest, skilled laborers, but a few will try to cheat you. A good contractor is invaluable, though. Seek his advice. You should be open to his suggestions, but not easily swayed away from your design's intent. Many disagreements between contractors and homeowners are the result of poor communications. Having clarified your ideas into a finished drawing will help alleviate these misunderstandings. A decent contractor is worthy of your respect. If you show your appreciation of his expertise, you will get a better job done.

The term "contractor" is actually a misnomer since many builders work without a contract. Their billings are computed on another basis. Excavation, for instance, is charged by the hour and masonry work is done by the block or brick. So the reluctance of a builder to draw up a contract does not necessarily mean he is unethical. If a good builder chooses not to work with a strict contract do not feel compelled to insist on one.

In any case, contractors will usually submit a cost estimate for your particular job in the form of a bid. Normally the contractor visits your site and either verbally or in writing presents a cost estimate for his services. Having several bids submitted on your job is a good idea. Not only will estimates vary, but by the time the second or third contractor has explained his bid you will have an understanding of what the job involves and what you *ought* to pay.

Obviously written estimates with breakdowns are best since they can be compared more easily. Written contracts can give you legal protection, too. With extensive work a written contract is preferable. In addition, you may want to set a mutually agreed upon ceiling—an upper limit—beyond which you would pay no more.

Check with neighbors who may have had similar work done and with local building supply houses for the names of reputable builders. And try to see examples of their workmanship. Actually word of mouth is the best reference a contractor can have. Weighing their reputations and their bids equally is probably the best way to hire a contractor.

Once a contractor has been chosen and work has begun, it is usually good policy to stay out of the way. There is a real difference between supervising the work and interfering. Only if you are paying by the hour need you keep close track of the work's progress. Otherwise let the workmen get on with it. Even if they appear to be wasting time don't complain to them, tell their boss first. It is his job to reprimand them, not yours. Also don't complain too quickly about their work. Many jobs look terrible until they are almost done. If you think that something is being done wrong, say so, but be sure of your ground. Ask questions and look up the job in illustrated building manuals before you angrily confront the contractor.

Delay in the contractor's work is the most common complaint of homeowners. Because of the bidding process and the fact that your job is probably a small one, some delays are almost inevitable. To survive a contractor must bid on many more jobs than he can handle and unless your job is large you will probably not be first on his list. A good (read busy) contractor is worth the wait, but if you feel you are being unfairly put off *politely* let him know of your annoyance. Visiting his other job sites to ask when he can be expected and leaving messages at the office have a cumulative effect. If you hound him enough without being nasty your work will get done before that of the less vocal clients.

GRADING

Major preliminary site work involves grading—both to fit the site to its new, proposed uses and to insure proper drainage. Most properties will require some grading, especially in those areas that have to be nearly level, such as foundations and drives. There are two types of grading. "Rough" grading is the movement of sub-surface soils. Today's earth-moving equipment can do this fairly quickly. The other, finish grading, refers to the replacement and fine grading of the topsoil only. Make sure that the topsoil is separated from the sub-surface material at the very start of excavation work and piled in a convenient, separate location. This is crucial since only topsoil is a growing medium for plants. Later, once the subsoil work has been completed, the topsoil should be replaced to the depth necessary to grow the proposed plant material. Too often contractors will indiscriminately mix the two and leave you with a yard incapable of nourishing vegetation beyond a few weeds.

Contractors also have a tendency to rough-grade a site without any regard to its future maintenance or aesthetics. This is particularly true in sub-division developments. Poorly done sub-surface grading is very difficult to correct once the topsoil has been replaced and vegetation planted. Grading work should be gentle and should conform to the surrounding terrain as much as possible. The transition from the new grades back into the undisturbed landforms ought to be smooth and gradual. It should look natural. Generally the best examples of grading are those where it is not immediately apparent any work has been done. Enough has been said elsewhere about the desirability of undulating landforms and earthworks, so do not be tempted to level every modulation on your site.

When major grading changes are anticipated, a grading plan drawn up by a competent engineer or landscape architect is essential. Professionally done, it will be sensitive to the landscape and explicitly self-explanatory to the contractor. The plan will be based on an accurate topographic survey. It shows both the existing and proposed contour lines and includes calculations of the amount of earth to be moved.

Sample grading plan

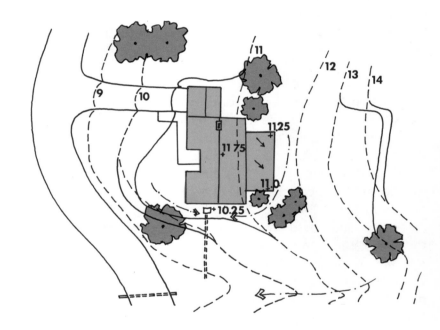

The object of these cut and fill calculations is to balance as far as possible the amount of soil added with the amount of soil cut away. This eliminates expensive off-site hauling. As has been mentioned before, extra soil offers excellent opportunities for building earthforms in the landscape.

In rough grading, it is important that the maximum acceptable grade for various activities be followed.

Abrupt grade changes are sometimes necessary in developing a property and can be well accommodated by walls and embankments. Retaining walls are attractive, interesting landscape features. They are also initially expensive (see Walls). Embank-

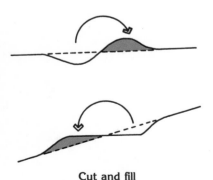

Cut and fill

MAXIMUM GRADES FOR SPECIFIC AREAS*

USE	GRADE	RATIO (horizontal to vertical)
Walks	8%	12:1
Ramps	20%	5:1
Ramps for handicapped	8%	12:1
Driveways	10%	10:1
Lawn	20%	5:1
Grass Bank	30%	3:1
Planted Bank	50%	2:1

* Ratio explanation: The first figure is the number of horizontal feet, the second is the vertical rise, so a ratio of 8:1 has one foot of vertical rise for every eight horizontal feet.

ments are far easier and cheaper to use, but they have maintenance disadvantages. Generally, earthen banks are limited to slopes of 2:1 or less; that is, two horizontal feet per vertical foot. If steep banks are used, they must be quickly covered and planted to prevent erosion. Slopes can be reinforced with railroad ties or stone rip-rap too (see Walls).

You can adjust sudden grade changes near trees with raised or lowered dry wells. Since this tends to look artificial and the

TREE WELLS

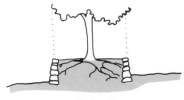

Raised

Lowered with tile drains

Lowered with loose stone infill for drainage

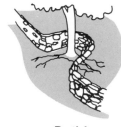

Partial

Recommended topsoil depths for different vegetation

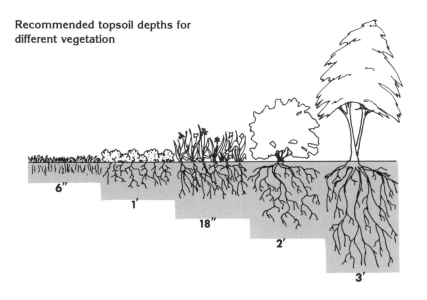

6"   1'   18"   2'   3'

trees' survival cannot be guaranteed, this is an extreme measure. Partial dry wells tend to be most pleasing in the landscape.

Since heavy equipment is required in subsurface grading, the average homeowner will be limited to working with the finish, topsoil grade. This is the final preparation of the ground to receive new plant materials and includes minor drainage work. The various depths of topsoil needed for different types of vegetation is important here. Obviously, the deeper the topsoil the richer the growing medium. The recommended depths are shown on page 117.

Before covering the subsurface work with topsoil, it is a good idea to break up and rake the compacted, subsurface soils. A rototiller will do this admirably. Once in place, the two soils should mix a little to insure the movement of water and nutrients between them.

DRAINAGE

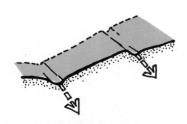

Swales or ditches at top and bottom of bank

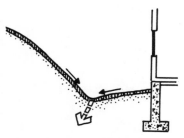

Swale between foundation and slope

Grading for drainage is necessary in site preparation, too. It insures that water is directed and carried away from the house area. Homes with perpetually flooding basements are mute testimony to its importance. Inadequate drainage can destroy the usefulness and appearance of a site and cause a myriad of annoying, expensive problems. The object is to be sure that water flows constantly, but slowly, across the land. Rapid run-off causes erosion and too sluggish movement results in wet spots.

The fundamental premise is simplicity itself: water runs downhill. While drainage systems can become complex, the average homeowner can usually do most of the work himself using a little common sense. Wherever possible water's natural movement downward should be facilitated by modestly sloping the finish grade work. Grades must always slope away from the house foundation. As we know, even seemingly flat areas have to have some grade to them. On a lawn or drive a slope of 1°-2° (one to two feet per 100) is unnoticeable to the eye, but provides decent drainage. It is normally best to channel surface waters into the land's natural drainage patterns. These natural drainage ways are termed swales and their pattern is very apparent after a heavy rain. Often man-made ditches, shallow and inconspicuously placed, can be used to feed run-off into these swales. A number of drainage problems can be solved this way.

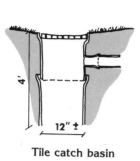

Tile catch basin

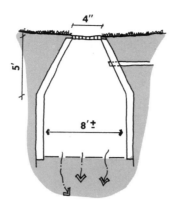

Concrete catch basin

Only when it becomes necessary to work temporarily against the natural flow must we turn to such devices as dry wells and catch basins. For draining small areas, dry wells and tile drains are more than adequate. They act as good collection points for gutter and downspout run-off as well.

Occasionally a site is subject to an off-site drainage nuisance or has severe problems because of heavy, impermeable soils. A property located at the base of a long hill may be flooded during storms and open to constant seepage. In such a situation, plants literally drown. A four-inch perforated drainpipe buried *across* the flow usually solves the problem by intercepting the water and channelling it out of harm's way. If impermeable soils or a bottom land site are the problem, it may be necessary to lay a whole system of pipes to maintain proper drainage. This involves subsurface work and must be done with heavy equipment.

Perforated pipe

CHAPTER 15

Obtaining and Transplanting Plants

BUYING, FINDING AND GROWING YOUR OWN

With the completion of: (1) site clearance where necessary, (2) subsurface grading, (3) installation of underground piping and wiring, (4) hard architectural features such as walks, drives, foundations, and terraces and (5) at least partial topsoil finish grading, you can begin to implement the planting plan. Planting, too, can be staged. Since large trees and shrubs are harder to move and form the backbone of most designs, they should be installed first. Medium shrubs, ground covers, and finally bulbs are planted next, usually in that order.

The homeowner has three options for obtaining plant material. He can buy it, find and transplant "wild" vegetation, or grow his own. They are not mutually exclusive. Someone may choose to pursue all three methods. Each has its own advantages and disadvantages.

Buying. Buying is the easiest and safest method. It can also be expensive. Whether you buy from a tree farm, a nursery, or garden center, several things should be considered. First, be sure of the firm's reputation. Ask around about it. The difference in quality and price between neighboring nurseries can be astonishing. Also ask for a copy of their plant catalogs. These will show the prices for various species and sizes available. They are an excellent way to comparison shop.

Take your planting plan or a plant list along on your shopping trips. *Never* go plant buying without a clear idea of at least the general characteristics of the plants you are after. That is analogous to going to the supermarket on an empty stomach. Plants are seductive and nurserymen are salesmen. It is far too easy to end up with a carload of beautiful "bargains" that are nevertheless expensive, and unsuitable for your design.

Their receptivity to your plan is a good indicator of the type of organization you are dealing with. They should be helpful and informative. Ask questions about your selections. What is the best time to transplant? What are its maintenance needs? "Plant people" are good people generally and they will be impressed when you come prepared. However, if a salesman tries to steer you to the specials, think twice about doing business there.

Most nurseries offer some form of a guarantee on their plant materials. It may vary considerably from place to place. Often the guarantee is dependent upon the nursery doing the planting as well. Allowing a nursery to perform guaranteed contract work deserves consideration. If your budget allows it and especially if large-sized plants have been specified, there are definite advantages. For one thing, it insures that the work will be done well. A six-month guarantee is the acceptable minimum. A year is better. It also spares you a great deal of heavy work. A particularly attractive alternative is limiting the guaranteed nursery work to the larger, more expensive items and doing the remainder yourself.

If you use guaranteed material which appears to be dying, don't wait until the last minute to notify the nursery. An early short note will avoid unpleasant complications later.

Always ask if they deliver plant materials to your home and what the rates are. This service is worth a reasonable fee since their equipment will allow the plants to be unloaded in place. Hauling numerous large trees and shrubs in the family sedan is a frustrating experience. With a little scheduling the planting holes can be ready when the delivery truck arrives and the job quickly done.

Plant materials are generally sold in four ways. "In the field" refers to plants you dig, move, and transplant yourself. Balled and burlaped species are ready to be transplanted immediately. Smaller shrubs are sometimes sold in metal or plastic containers. Also, occasionally, very small hardy species are offered "bare root." Balled and burlaped or container-grown plants are usually the best for non-gardeners.

Regardless of how the vegetation is being sold, pick out the individual plants you want from among those offered. Look for healthy new growth and strong branching patterns. A few dead or wilted leaves does not necessarily mean a dying plant. However, if the entire plant shows signs of yellowing or gashed and broken branches are apparent, move on to others. With balled and burlaped plants always check the ball to see that it is firm and in one piece. Broken earthen balls can mean root damage. When a particularly fine tree or shrub is called for in your plan, ask to see their specimens. These should be the exceptional examples of each variety.

There are other outlets for plant materials. Mail order houses and department store specials are just two. Undoubtedly there are price bargains to be found. Again, however, the temptation may be to allow these "bargains" to determine what you select in the way of plant material. Don't buy on impulse. Stay within the set of characteristics you have developed for your different plant types. If you come across a sale of appropriate species, by all means take advantage of it, but be wary. These plants are often bargains in name only.

Digging Your Own. Plant materials found in a wild state can also be used. This is an especially good way to augment costly plant purchases. All you need are a plant identification guide book, a sense of adventure, and *permission.* Uncultivated, but attractive varieties of trees and shrubs may exist elsewhere within your property, on a friend's land, or on any other property whose owner offers his permission.

The search should cover at least two separate areas. Local plants can be found in their natural habitats and more ornamental species can often be located on development sites. Abandoned house sites are almost always surrounded by the remains of gardens. Whether you are plant hunting in a rural area or searching around a construction site, *be sure to ask for permission.* If you ask politely and clean up after yourself landowners usually won't deny permission. Removing plants from public or private lands without the owner's consent is theft, but being able to utilize plant materials that are not nursery-grown is an asset.

Plant material hunts are enjoyable outings and the advantage of finding "free" plants is obvious. It is riskier, though, and more time-consuming than visiting a nursery. During the procedure of digging up, moving and transplanting some plant material will be lost.

Nevertheless, with proper handling many varieties will make the move easily. Generally the smaller in size the plant material is the better. The main difference between a nursery-grown plant and a wild one is that the nursery plant has been periodically root-pruned so that transplanting is less traumatic for it. This does not mean you are limited to moving ground covers and small shrubs. A six to eight foot tree is usually no problem.

The success of wild transplants rests on two factors: the first is the gentle, proper handling of the plant throughout the procedure; the second is providing the plant with an environment similar to the one in which it was found. This means that if the plant was originally growing in a sunny location it ought to be transplanted to a sunny spot. The same is true of wet soils, shady locations, and other growing conditions. This will greatly lessen the plant's trauma and increase its chances for survival.

The seasonal timing for transplanting is important, too. In temperate climates most deciduous trees and shrubs are best transplanted in the early spring. Evergreen plants are usually moved in late fall before the ground freezes.

Growing Your Own. The homeowner can also grow his own plant material. This method is generally better for the more horticulturally-inclined person than for the average homeowner, however. It is a rewarding experience, but the young plants will have to be carefully tended for a number of years before they can be effective in the landscape.

The weekend gardener has several avenues for growing material. He can either obtain very young plants through nurseries, mail order houses, or the Forest Service, or he can propagate from existing plant materials or from seeds.

The Forest Service, by the way, offers young trees in large quantities at very low prices to property owners. If you own a rural piece of property and are prepared to wait for these seedlings to mature, contact their nearest office for more information.

Propagating plants is done in three ways: layering, cutting, and grafting. Layering and cutting are by far the easiest for the amateur. In addition, more trees and shrubs can be propagated by these two methods than by grafting. All three methods produce plants with the same exact characteristics as the parent plant. This is not true of seed-propagated plants which have the characteristics of both parents.

There is not space here to go into the details of each method. Suffice it to say that a fair amount of work is involved and several years are needed before the plant material can be used. Nevertheless, it can be a rewarding experience, particularly if it is pursued after your landscape is basically developed. Numerous excellent books are available on propagation if you are interested.

TRANSPLANTING

First the location for the new plant must be decided upon. Only then can you go and get them. The outlined procedure applies to both deciduous and evergreen trees and shrubs.

Transplanting requires coordination and preparation. You will need to have:
—a suitable means to transport the material
—holes already dug and ready to receive the new material
—fertilizer, peat moss conveniently placed
—water available; hoses that reach the newly dug holes is best
—at least one helper
—tools: shovel, picks, a knife, and pruning tools
—material to wrap and cover the plants.

Temporary conditions can exist that may make it wise to postpone transplanting vegetation. These would include: waterlogged soils, subsurface frost, drought, or strong, dry winds. Any of these passing conditions will lessen the chances of successful transplants.

PROCEDURE FOR TRANSPLANTING FOUND PLANTS

Digging. Once you have located a plant, begin digging a trench all the way around the trunk or stem. Allow at least one foot between the plant and the trench for every inch of diameter in the trunk. For example, a small dogwood one and a half inches in diameter at waist height will require an eighteen-inch digging radius. Using a shovel or pick, dig down and underneath the plant. You should dig a minimum of eighteen inches deep. Continue around until the plant is nearly dislodged. The idea is to save as many of the roots, especially the tiny hair roots, as possible. Obviously some roots will have to be cut. Try to leave as much soil attached to the remaining roots as possible. You are making a plant ball.

With the tree or shrub nearly loose, gently push the plant down to one side and finish digging it out. Lift the plant carefully out of the hole by picking up the root and soil ball. *Never* pull up on the stem or branches. (Be sure to fill in the hole before you leave, too.)

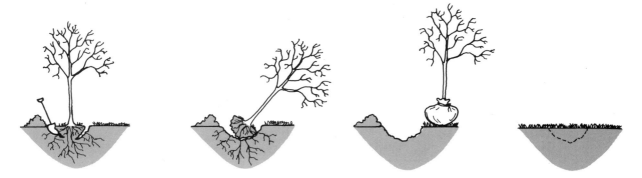

Moving. Next, secure the roots by wrapping the soil ball in a plastic garbage bag, tarp, burlap, or similar material. Occasionally this is done while the plant is still in the ground. If the wrapping material can be forced around and under the ball, so much the better because it can then be used to lift the tree or shrub out of the ground with less chance of damage to its root system.

If possible, wet the bag a little, too. This will prevent the roots from drying out during the trip back to your house. Covering the leaves and trunk with a light plastic sheet or something similar is also a good preventive measure. If a truck is being used, you can cover the entire open section instead of covering each plant individually. Root damage and dry-out from sun and wind are the main problems in moving plant materials. So check to see that the plants are in a stable transporting position and are well covered. Drive carefully. Needless jostling will break up the earth balls. This applies to purchased balled and burlaped material, too.

Plants that are not being replanted immediately should be temporarily set aside in the shade and watered lightly. The less time they remain in transit between sites the better.

Transplanting. The hole you have dug already to receive the plant should be at least one to two feet wider and a foot deeper than the plant's earthen ball. These measurements are not a fast rule, but when in doubt go bigger than you might think necessary.

Before you set the new plant in, thoroughly water the hole itself. The sides and bottom should be soaked to the point where small puddles form that do not immediately drain away. Next add a healthy layer (24 inches) of peat moss. Sometimes a 50/50 mixture of peat moss and sand or peat with a little cured manure is added instead. If you are planting nursery-bought materials ask them what planting mixture they recommend for the particular plants. Otherwise, straight peat moss is best.

Whatever is added must be watered and packed down. The easiest way to compress it is to step on it. Wear old shoes and work clothes!

Now the plant itself can be set into the hole. Again you should be lifting and lowering the plant by the soil ball, not the branches or trunk. Be sure the plant is standing straight up before you begin to fill the hole in. Also you may want to turn it until the best side faces in the direction you want. Remember that the plant must always set at the same level or a little deeper than where it grew before. That is, the stem or trunk should surface at the same spot it did before.

Next, remove the material used to wrap the soil ball. If burlap is used, cut and roll it down the sides of the root ball. While a heavy, impenetrable material has to be totally removed, burlap does not because it will decompose and not hinder the passage of roots or moisture. Nurseries are increasingly using a woven plastic material on plant balls. Some of this can be allowed to remain on the plant if it is difficult to remove totally. Cut and remove as much as possible, though.

If the plant is in a container of any kind it also will have to be removed. Usually these can be cut or torn away easily. With metal containers, tap on the bottom until the compacted root ball comes out.

No matter how the root ball is contained, it must be handled gently. Try to hold it together at all costs.

Begin backfilling around the plant using a mixture of good topsoil and organic matter. The ratio is usually one part organic matter, peat moss or otherwise, to three parts topsoil. As you do this, work in and around the root system tamping the soil mixture with your hand or foot. Take care that no air pockets exist.

After filling in the hole, tamp the soil once more with your feet and water *thoroughly* again. With your feet make a slight depression around the plant to collect water. It should be a saucer shape and you may want to add a little additional organic material inside it. This will act as a mulch to conserve moisture during dry spells.

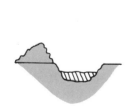 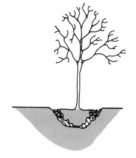 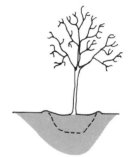

"Found" trees and shrubs will have to be pruned back at this point. Approximately thirty percent of the topgrowth must be removed to compensate for the trauma and root-loss of the transplanting operation. Occasional minor pruning may be necessary on nursery-bought plant stock as well. This is especially true if the root ball is damaged in transplanting. Look to the maintenance section for detailed pruning instructions.

Staking. Large trees need to be staked temporarily for support. Two by two inch hardwood stakes serve well for this. The stakes must be driven in until they are securely in place and must still be long enough to reach beyond the bottom branches. They should be driven in about four to six inches from the tree. Trees with a trunk diameter of less than two inches usually need only one stake. A single stake always belongs on the windward side of the tree. Two to four inch diameter trees require two stakes. Anything larger than that is very rare in the do-it-yourself home landscape

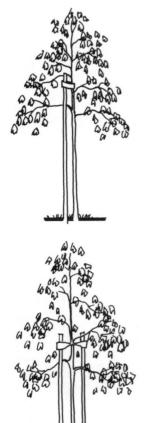

for the simple reason that it is just too big to handle without equipment.

Bind the stakes to the tree with wire run through cut sections of old garden hosing. Heavy cord or clothesline are less desirable, but adequate substitutes. It is important that the thin outer bark of the young trees not be damaged in any way. Don't use wire or any other material that will gouge and cut into the trees. Crossing the rope or hose between the tree and the stake will lessen unnecessary abrasion.

Planting ordered bare root material and small "found" plants deserve special attention here.

It is not normally recommended that you buy any plants bare root, since a high percentage of them will probably not survive. However, if you have, the planting procedure is slightly different. Any dried-out, withered, or broken roots should be pruned off the moment the shrubs are unwrapped. In addition one third of the top growth must be cut away as well. This allows the plant to concentrate its strength in a few remaining branches. Finally, during the planting procedure be sure to spread out the roots of the bare-rooted plant within the planting hole.

Small found plants such as ground covers, ferns, and even wildflowers can be transplanted by following the same planting procedure outlined for trees and shrubs. Newspapers can be used to wrap the root systems.

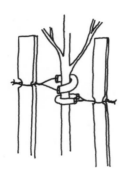

Watering. Watering is the essential last step in transplanting. Moderate or insufficient watering is probably the single most prominent cause of transplant failure. New trees and shrubs need to be watered frequently and thoroughly for several months. The intervals and amount of water to apply vary depending upon rainfall and drainage. Under normal weather conditions, though, new plants ought to be watered at least once a week in the hotter months. During the first few weeks they will require it twice as often. Thoroughly watering is more than just a sprinkling. The leaves and stems should be sprayed and the area around the base of the plant should be soaked until small puddles appear on the surface. It can be overdone—too much water will drown a plant. Most homeowners, though, do not do it nearly enough and are then at a loss to explain why their new plants are dying. So please, water your plants!

CHAPTER 16

Maintenance

Nature is always in a state of flux. Left to itself, any controlled landscape will eventually return to a natural, wild condition. Maintenance is essential to hold this urge in check. It is a follow-through on your design, ensuring that the landscape develops and matures into the attractive, usable space you envisioned.

No landscape is totally maintenance-free. Even asphalt eventually needs attention. Most of you will have to be prepared to do this maintenance work yourselves. Paying the neighborhood boy to mow the lawn or contracting with a maintenance firm can lessen the burden, but even so, the supervision and detail work will inevitably fall on you.

THE LOW MAINTENANCE LANDSCAPE

It is possible to minimize maintenance requirements, however, and to plan ahead for a low-maintenance landscape. The growing trend toward more informal lifestyles and just plain economic reasons have caused great interest in limiting property upkeep. Low maintenance begins in the initial planning phase. Everything should be designed with maintenance in mind. Then it must be executed with care, using quality construction materials. The expense of doing it well the first time is an investment in low upkeep. Shoddy workmanship, ill-conceived designs, and poor-quality materials guarantee trouble later.

Since the majority of maintenance work revolves around plant materials, we will concentrate on those problems.

HINTS FOR LOW MAINTENANCE

Remember when choosing plants to select those which require little special care and are naturally hardy in your area.

Cut down on or eliminate sheared and trimmed plant materials from your design. For example, a formal hedge requires constant pruning, whereas a group of unpruned shrubs, or better yet, a fence, might do the job equally well.

Use mulches of all kinds to lessen constant, backbreaking weeding.

Grass-covered areas should be designed as open lawns with few shrubs and trees to mow around. So try not to plant individual trees and shrubs within lawn areas. Mowing is the number one maintenance item in most landscapes. Grass is usually worth the trouble, but at least consider your mower's maneuverability when laying out grass areas. Avoid sharp corners, tight hard-to-reach spots, and grass "islands." These areas ought to be given over to mulches, groundcovers or shrubs.

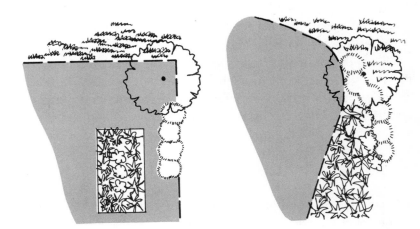

Rectangular, cut up lawn changed to curved bed with plantings out of lawn area and meadow grass beyond.

If your property includes large open lawns, consider allowing some of them to revert to meadow. Such areas are pleasant to look at and need to be mowed only once or twice a year to discourage underbrush.

Built-in sprinkler systems are a fine idea for very dry climates where perpetual watering is inevitable. (Ideally, you would consider low-maintenance alternatives instead. Lawns can be replaced with drought-resistant ground covers; mulches and arid-loving plants can be used.)

Transition between lawn and meadow grass is here emphasized by slope.

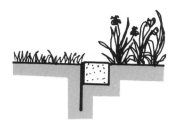 

Mowing strips—brick and concrete edging. They allow the mower to cut the edges of the lawn cleanly.

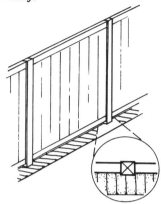

Mowing strip—along fence (brick)

Mowing "strips" will eliminate tedious edging work. Planting beds, trees, fences, and walls can all accommodate mowing strips. Numerous materials can be used. Concrete, brick and metal are the most familiar. While they may seem a little overbearing when installed, time quickly makes them less apparent.

Have ready access to the appropriate maintenance tools. Using the correct labor-saving device for the job and having it within easy reach saves enormous amounts of time. Also be sure that hoses can reach to all parts of the garden and that wheelbarrows and other equipment can maneuver easily about the grounds.

Give up the suburban mania for perfect lawns. Putting green textures require full-time attendants. A serviceable, attractive lawn should have several types of grass in it. A few weeds need not drive you to distraction. (See Lawn Care.)

The following sections will deal with specific maintenance needs in detail.

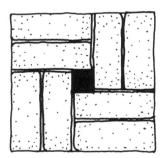

Pole or lightpost mowing strip—brick

Most properties need some soil modification and fertilizers are the simplest means of altering soil characteristics. The fertilizer to be used depends on the existing soil conditions and the site's vegetation. Two neighboring properties will never have identical fertilizer needs. Soil conditions can vary considerably over short distances and plant species have differing pH requirements for maximum growth. Time and budget considerations will also influence the choice between fertilizer types and methods. Some are simpler to apply or less expensive than others.

Your soil should have been analyzed as a part of Step

FERTILIZERS

3—Identifying Existing Conditions. If this was not done, don't hesitate any longer. Soil characteristics can be easily determined with an inexpensive soil testing kit or, better yet, by contacting the county Extension Service. This governmental agency will analyze soil samples and offer useful advice free of charge. The results of the test will help you choose between the wide range of available fertilizer types and formulations.

Fertilizers are generally used to increase the nutrient content, improve soil texture, and to affect the pH level (the alkaline-acid relationship). Speaking in very broad terms, soil problems usually fall into one of three major categories: acidic soils, high sand or clay content, or low nutrient soils.

TYPES OF FERTILIZERS

	Chemical	Organic Fertilizer	Organic Matter
Ease of application	Easiest to spread on both soil and grass	Must be raked into soil, but can be spread onto grass.	Should be mixed with soil, can be spread onto grass at the end of the growing season.
Cost	Expensive	Less expensive	Least expensive (free if you have animals or compost)
Use in conjunction with lime	Apply before	Apply with or before	Apply with or before
Moisture holding capacity	None	Moderate	Excellent
Soil texture improvement	None	Moderate	Excellent
Rate of penetration	Rapid	General	Slow
Duration of effectiveness	Short-term (3-4 years before reapplication)	Slightly longer	Semi-permanent improvement
Ecological Impact	Severe. Can destroy helpful soil bacteria and earthworms and is potentially harmful to plants and wildlife; use sparingly. Over-application will kill vegetation.	Slight, although some harm is possible if over-applied.	Positive impact, no ecological drawbacks. Encourages soil bacteria and is not harmful if overapplied.
Foreign substances seeds, etc.	Contains no foreign substances.	May contain a few undesirable seeds.	Will contain some weed seeds.

Acidic soils are readily corrected by adding lime. While not a true fertilizer, lime as an alkaline substance will lower the acid content of the soil to a suitable level. It is an especially important ingredient in a healthy lawn. (See Lawn Care.) Occasionally with acid-loving plants such as rhododendron, it is necessary to increase soil acidity. This is best done by spreading sulphur, ferrous sulphate, or aluminum sulphate in the immediate vicinity of those plants.

With high sand and clay content soils the problems are primarily texture and drainage, although they tend to have a low nutrient value as well. These conditions can be improved by thoroughly mixing organic matter into the top four to six inches soil. Peat moss and manure are the two most popular forms of humus or organic matter.

Poor quality soils will need to have their nutrient content raised with a combination of added organic matter and organic or chemical fertilizer. In extreme cases, it may be necessary to haul better quality topsoil from another site.

Fertilizers themselves have three main classifications: chemical, organic fertilizer, and organic matter. Chemical fertilizers contain raw soil nutrients in the form of nitrogen, phosphate, and potash. They have no organic material whatsoever. Commercial organic fertilizers are composed of a mixture of humus, usually manure, and chemical additives. Organic matter is natural, unadulterated humus. There are numerous advantages and disadvantages to each type.

When buying fertilizers at your local hardware or garden supply house, be sure to ask questions and read the labels and directions thoroughly. Chemical fertilizers are labeled by the percentage of nitrogen, phosphate, and potash they contain. Thus a 5/10/5 mixture would contain five percent nitrogen, ten percent phosphate and five percent potash. The optimum time to apply and the amount called for is dependent upon your growing season and the plants to be fertilized. Generally early spring is the best time to fertilize. Do not apply it at the end of the growing season. This forces new, easily-damaged shoots which will probably not survive the colder or dormant period.

No matter what fertilizer is used, it should always be applied over the entire root area. This root area of a tree or shrub extends at least to its "drip-line."

Shrub dripline

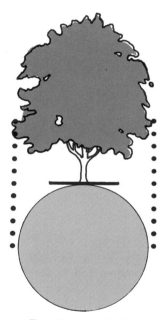

Tree feeding, dripline

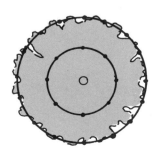

Feeding holes and position

Trees are fed by applying fertilizer into a series of equidistant twelve to fifteen inch deep holes drilled midway between the trunk and drip-line and again at the drip-line. Fifteen holes for every inch in the tree trunk's diameter are recommended. Many people use a stake or metal pipe to hammer out the feed holes.

LAWN MAINTENANCE

Because lawns are usually the last thing to be laid out and are the most time-consuming in terms of maintenance, their installation and early care will be treated here.

Lawns form the major open spaces in most domestic landscapes and serve as the necessary balance to more heavily planted areas. They are highly visible and often heavily used. They are also a traditional and well-loved part of the American home.

Fortunately, grass is a low-budget item that is relatively easy for the homeowner to install. In fact, it is probably the least expensive commercially available plant material. In terms of its pleasant, immediate effects and its function as a green carpet in your outdoor space—it is a bargain. It is a high maintenance item, however, and the use of edges and mowing strips is encouraged. (See Low-Maintenance Hints.) In the average home, though, its high upkeep is worthwhile as long as the owner does not have a fetish for putting greens. The perfect lawn is an elusive and burdensome goal at best and a nearly impossible one for the weekend gardener.

The best way to guarantee an attractive, manageable lawn is to: prepare the soil well, choose the correct grass type or mixture, and install it properly.

Regardless of the planting method or the type(s) of grass used, the topsoil must be well prepared. Ideally this means cultivating the soil to a depth of six to eight inches with a rototiller. Organic materials can be added at this point. Earthen clumps should be broken up and rocks raked out. If your soil test is acidic, lime can be added to provide a more suitable pH level. Then the topsoil should be smoothed to the finish grade level. All the little depressions and bumps need to be leveled to get a flowing, even lawn.

Selecting the appropriate grass type and planting method is

It's easy to make tools for smoothing topsoil to the finish grade.

Drag planks

Flat rake

the very important next step. Whereas the poor choice of a shrub need not destroy the total effect of a garden, a shoddy, unhealthy lawn can.

Nearly forty domestic grasses are used for lawns in this country. The best selection for you depends on climate, site conditions, soil characteristics and on the anticipated traffic the grass must bear. Usually a commercial mixture of three or four different grass types is recommended for seeded lawns. Each has its own characteristics and tolerances. A mixture is safer than relying on only one type since it will be better able to withstand extreme conditions and diseases. In time the grasses most suitable to your particular site will come to dominate the lawn. Mixtures with more than six seed types are usually unsatisfactory, though, as they tend to result in lawns that are "spotty" in color and texture.

Grass can be installed several ways. Seeding is by far the most common residential method and will be concentrated on here. However, grass can also be transplanted as plugs, sprigs, stalons and rolled sod. Transplanted grasses are used primarily in the Deep South and Southwest and are usually termed warm-season grasses. The Zoysia and Bermuda species are among those often transplanted. If you are considering transplanted varieties, the nursery or sod farm where you purchase the grass will be able to explain the best installation procedure for your particular variety and site.

No matter what method of installation you choose, ask lots of questions as you shop around. *Always* purchase your grass or seed mixtures from reputable companies. With seed mixtures be sure to read the directions carefully. Check labels for allowable noxious weed content and note the area covered per pound. Your to-scale design will allow you to calculate correctly the square footage of the proposed lawn area, so you will know how much seed is necessary.

When choosing between seed mixtures pay particular attention to the proportion of fine textured species to coarse ones. In general, the coarser varieties are hardier, more durable, grow faster, are more tolerant of extreme conditions and will need less maintenance. Fine textured grasses form tighter, more perfect lawns, but tend to be slow-growers, less wear resistant, intolerant of extreme conditions (shade, cold, soil) and harder to maintain.

Fine Seed Grasses

All bent grass varieties, fine fescues (Creeping Red, Chewings and Ranier) and all bluegrasses

Coarse Seed Grasses

Red top, clover, alta and meadow fescues, and perennial and annual rye grasses

The correct proportion of coarse to fine grasses depends on the particulars of your site, the anticipated use of the lawn areas and maintenance considerations.

Planting the Seed. Once a seed mixture is selected it can be sown onto the prepared topsoil with mechanical spreaders or by hand. Renting or borrowing a mechanical spreader is recommended as hand-sown grass is usually uneven. Gently rake over the seeded areas to mix the seed into the loose soil. Do this very lightly. Next, roll the seeded lawn with a roller to bind the soil and seed together. This should be done twice from different directions. Rollers are also easy to rent in most areas. The final crucial step is watering. The seeded area must be thoroughly, but gently, watered once the planting procedure is completed and again several times until the grass is firmly established. Special care should be taken to see that the new lawn stays slightly moist, as young grass shoots will wither quickly under dry conditions. A lawn can be considered established and mowable when the grass reaches one and a half to two inches.

An unnecessary movement across the new tender lawn should be avoided for the first few weeks. Fence the area off if need be. Occasionally burlap cloth or other anti-erosion nets are used as an added precaution on new lawns. They are especially useful on newly seeded banks and slopes to hold the young growth in place. If you use them do not attempt to remove them once the grass is established, but allow them to rot in place.

PRUNING

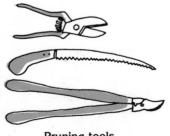

Pruning tools

Pruning is a part of any regular home maintenance program and is something anyone can do. Trees and shrubs, particularly deciduous ones, will sometimes require an occasional pruning to remove undesirable growth. Pruning is also an excellent early step in rejuvenating older landscapes. It results in healthier, more attractive vegetation by:

—removing dead, dying, diseased and damaged branches,

—correctively shaping plants—especially older, overgrown ones,

—increasing the size and number of blooms,

—forcing new, fuller growth,

—creating formal shapes where appropriate, such as in sheared hedges and topiary.

As a rule, all plants should be carefully pruned to keep their natural shape. The only exceptions are plants that are being purposely shaped for formal or decorative reasons.

Proper and improper hedge pruning. Widening the bottom of the hedge allows adequate rain and sunlight to reach it.

Formal and informal shrub pruning

Most plants can be pruned anytime of the year without lasting ill effect. Usually though, coniferous (evergreen) varieties are best pruned in the early spring when new growth is just beginning. Deciduous shrubs are generally pruned according to their flowering period. Spring flowering shrubs are pruned in the late spring *after* their blooms have faded and summer flowering shrubs in late winter *before* new growth has begun. This sequence is only important in insuring that the shrubs' seasonal flower display will not be interrupted or reduced by the pruning. If you are still apprehensive about when to prune a particular species, contact a local nursery or the Extension Service for further advice.

For the average homeowner pruning is a simple means to improve his plants. Overgrown trees and shrubs can be trimmed into pleasant shapes and older woody plants can be rejuvenated by cutting them back to force new growth. How you prune determines the future shape of the plant.

Older shrubs can be renewed by severely cutting back the old main stems to near ground level. Thinning out the old wood from fast growing, multi-stemmed shrubs on a yearly basis is a sound maintenance practice as well. It will keep the shrub in bounds and assure vigorous growth and flowering every season.

Pruning for shape: upright and wide open growth

Pruning back: cut out older main stems near the ground. Don't just cut across the top.

About one-third of the older wood stems should be removed each year. Old growth is easily recognized by its size and dark, rougher bark.

Occasionally the opposite approach is taken with large, mature shrubs. Rather than removing or cutting them back, they can be pruned up to give the appearance of small trees. This is an attractive way to open up an overgrown garden corner and still maintain an interesting, mature shrub.

Pruning up a tree

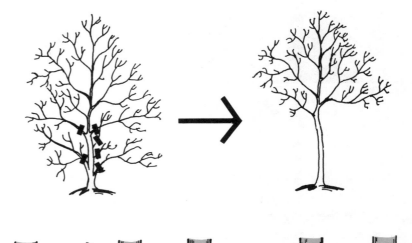

(A) Removing tree branches: cuts #1, 2, & 3
(B) Don't leave stubs or cut into the main trunk.

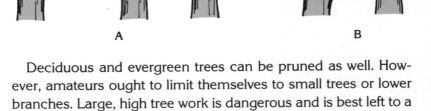

A   B

Deciduous and evergreen trees can be pruned as well. However, amateurs ought to limit themselves to small trees or lower branches. Large, high tree work is dangerous and is best left to a reputable arborist.

Large branches within reach can be removed with a pruning saw. The final cut should always be flush. Stubs or gouges are both unsightly and potentially damaging to the tree. If you are pruning up a trunk by removing lower branches it should be done gradually. Usually four to five feet a year is the maximum.

Small coniferous trees and shrubs can also be contained by periodic root pruning or by cutting the top leader. Root pruning

Cutting the leader

slows the plant's rate of growth. It is done by simply cutting the roots around the tree or shrub with a shovel about one-third of the distance in from the plant's outer branches. Early spring is the best time to root prune. This works well on small trees or shrubs, particularly firs, cedars, spruces, and junipers. To keep coniferous plants shorter and fuller cut the lead shoot or top leader. This can permanently dwarf the plant so only consider it where absolutely necessary. It is normally used to maintain the desired height and density of evergreen hedges.

Newly transplanted, found plant materials must always be heavily pruned as part of the transplanting procedure. The same is true of bought bare root species. Usually one-third of the top growth of either shrub or trees should be cut back. This allows the smaller, traumatized root system to support the remaining leaves without straining. Cut only the minor, imperfect branches and leave the basic shape of the tree or shrub alone. *Never* cut the leader or central stem unless you mean to dwarf it permanently.

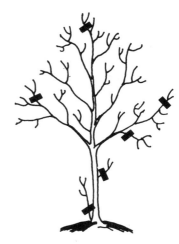

Prune out only the less desirable branches on a newly transplanted tree.

—Wounds of over one inch in diameter should be treated as soon as possible to avoid decay and later disease and insect problems. Tree dressings are commercially available, inexpensive, and easy to apply with a brush. The best are usually antiseptic asphalt varnishes.

—Never cut the lead shoot (the central stem) unknowingly.

—All cuts should be made at slight angle, not straight on.

—When pruning out deadwood make your cut at least one inch into the remaining live branch.

—Minor pruning is generally done with pruning shears or lopping shears. These tools should be sharp to ensure a clean cut. With either tool, cut completely through the wood in one smooth motion. Bending and twisting as you cut results in torn, rough wounds that will take longer to heal.

—As you prune, step back occasionally to study the plant's form and your progress. Good pruning is a little like sculpting—you are creating a more perfect shape. So don't indiscriminately lop off limbs and branches!

PRUNING HINTS

WATERING

Watering plant material is crucial during dry periods. The soil must be thoroughly saturated, not sprinkled. Applications should be long and gentle and done preferably in the late afternoon or early evening. The moisture can then be retained overnight instead of evaporating in the hot sun. Avoid frequent, light sprinklings as this will cause the plant to develop a shallow, unstable root structure. Turn to the transplanting procedure for more watering information.

MULCHES

Mulching around and under trees and shrubs has several benefits. Mulches can:
—suppress weed growth and reduce maintenance,
—protect plant material by modifying soil temperatures, keeping it warmer in winter and cooler in summer,
—retain moisture,
—improve soil quality by adding organic material,
—attractively outline and designate planting beds.

Mulching around an entryway

Many organic mulches are available at little or no expense. Grass clippings, rotting sawdust, rain-damaged hay, loose straw, leaf mold, wood chips, and bark shreds are all fine mulch materials. A two to four inch layer of any one of these will do the job. For the best results the mulch layers should be renewed by adding a little new material once or twice a season.

When spreading an organic mulch do not allow it to touch the plant itself as it may burn the plant during decomposition. Wood chips, sawdust, and bark also tend to deplete soil nitrogen as they decompose, Adding a half pound of sodium nitrate to each bushel of mulch will alleviate this problem.

The best of all the organic mulches, compost, can be produced in your backyard by composting left-over kitchen and plant materials. Composting creates a nutrient-rich mulch and is a sound ecological practice. For more information on composting contact your Extension Service for pamphlets and turn to the bibliography.

Flat, crushed rock and river pebbles also make excellent mulches, although they can add no organic material to the soil. Along with wood chips and bark, they make the most attractive mulches. A one to three inch layer of stones makes a permanent mulch. Used in conjunction with black polyethylene sheets they can virtually eliminate weeding. Six millimeter plastic sheets of polyethylene are available at most hardware and building supply outlets.

Mulching of any kind will lesson the maintenance care of almost any plant material. Even without using polyethylene, the occasional weeds that poke through can be easily removed or controlled with weed killers. In addition, the effect of weed-free, clean mulch lines and borders in and around plants will enhance the garden. The natural colors of stone, wood chips or composted materials all fit well in the home landscape.

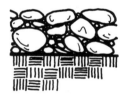

Pebbles, 6 mm. polyethylene sheet, soil

APPENDIX

Exercises

The following eight projects were designed for the use of *Homeowners Guide to Landscape Design* as a textbook. Specifically, they are for use in semester-length classes in continuing or adult education courses and at colleges and junior colleges.

All of the projects relate directly back to the steps described in the book. They can be done after you have completed the pertinent chapters or after you have read the whole text.

Whether you are enrolled in a course or not, the projects will help you a great deal in understanding landscape design and in preparing your own landscape plan.

Project 1: Reading the Land

Objective: To gain a better understanding of your property and to begin working in measured plan drawings.

Take a Fresh Look. Before we begin to design a landscape plan we need to take a fresh look at the property. Step 1 asks you to do just that.

You are asked to spend an hour or so just walking around and looking at the property, *as it exists.* Don't begin thinking about design solutions, but just look!

It is suggested that you:

1. Bring a compass to accurately locate the four cardinal directions North, South, East, and West. You may be surprised.

2. Take notes on what you see to be the property's assets and problems and any special features or characteristics.

3. Take a few selected slides or photographs of the house and property to refer back to. Be sure to develop them soon. You will need them in Project 5.

Project 2: Making a Base Map

Objective: To produce an accurate map of your property.

All other drawings and the final landscape plan will be taken off this original base map, so it is very important that this map be produced with care.

By following the instructions in Chapter 3 you will be able to measure and locate all the key items on your property. The base map will need to include at least these items.

- North arrow
- Property lines
- Location of the house corners
- Entrances
- Walkways
- Driveway
- Terraces and patios
- Major trees, shrubs and planting beds. (For clarity show existing trees and shrubs like so ⊙ . Evergreens are sometimes shown as ✳ . Later, with proposed vegetation, a + instead of a dot is used.)
- Other landscape features

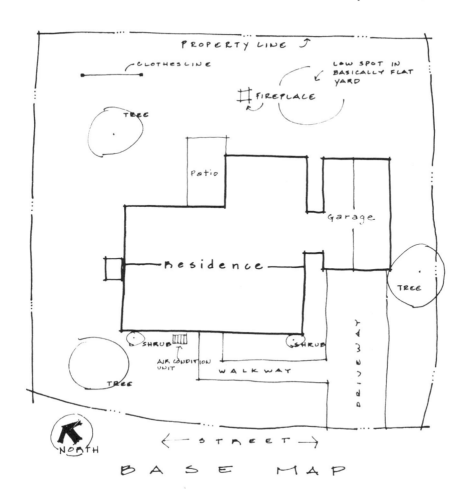

With a 17 × 22-inch graph paper sheet and using the 1 inch-equals-10-feet scale described on page 17, you can draw a property 170 × 220 feet. If your whole property will not fit, either go to a larger sheet of graph paper or confine your drawing to an area 170 × 220 feet, so long as it includes the portion of your landscape you are most concerned with.

Project 3: Existing Conditions Map. What do you have to work with?

Objective: To identify and locate all of the existing conditions on your property.

By overlaying a piece of tracing paper on the prepared base map or with a xeroxed copy of it, graphically depict the existing conditions.

Refer back to the site analysis checklist of possible items in Chapter 4. The notes you took as part of Step 1 may come in handy now. Remember that *existing conditions* means both the assets *and* liabilities of the particular property. After all, it is not *all* bad. Note the good things, too.

As in the example shown here, the good and bad conditions need to be located roughly on the existing conditions map *and* identified in writing.

This is not a finished drawing, but a landscape design tool. It can and should be loose in nature, not hard-lined or precise. And write all over it. The written notes will help you later.

The drawing should address at least these things:

- Orientation to the sun
- Notes on climatic, seasonal problems, such as terrace too hot in summer, drive hard to snow plow, too windy, and so on.
- Wind directions, if known
- Good, bad, or potential views
- Steep slopes and/or poor drainage spots
- And *lots* of brief comments on how *you* feel about both the property as a whole, both its individual pieces and their relationship to each other.

EXERCISE

For those of you who are interested in landscaping for solar energy gain this little additional exercise can be helpful in getting you started.

Reproduce the sun azimuth shown on page 24 and superimpose it on the north arrow shown on your maps. It will give a good idea of the seasonal arcs of the sun over your property. Remember the azimuth is for latitude 38°. The farther north or south your property is from 38°, the higher or lower the seasonal arcs of the sun will be.

The information is useful in planning both the home itself and its surroundings. The sun is the basic determinant of your particular climate. If the climate is cold, you need to plan to let in as much sunlight as possible and locate terraces and greenhouses accordingly. If it is hot, consider shade trees, trellises, and so on. Overhangs can be designed to let in wanted winter sun and shade out hot summer sun (see sketch, page 24).

Judicious landscaping planning of the home can save up to 30 percent of a residence's heating and cooling energy needs. Landscaping can do it attractively, too. Earth is the world's least expensive insulating material and, other than the ocean, plants are the greatest climate modifier. So begin to consider energy-conscious design features in your landscape plan.

Start thinking of both plants and earthforms as climate modifiers. As you begin approaching your final design in the next project, remember that they can offer shade, block winter's winds, funnel cool breezes, and conserve energy by creating protected areas around the home.

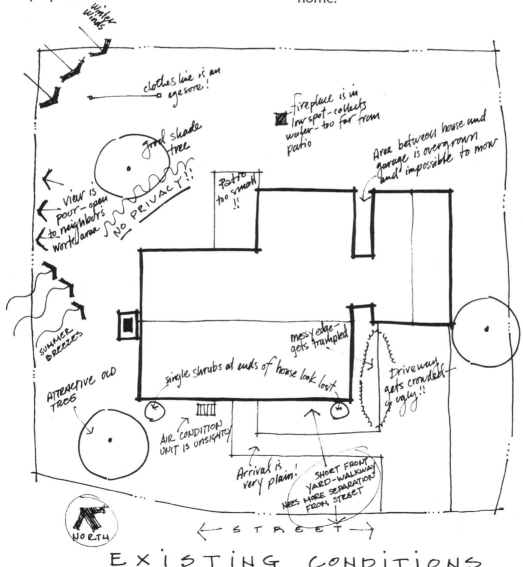

Winter winds

clothes line is an eyesore!

fireplace is in low spot—collects water—too far from patio

good shade tree

Area between house and garage is overgrown and impossible to mow

view is poor—open to neighbor's work area

NO PRIVACY!!

Patio too small!!

messy edge—gets trampled

summer breezes

single shrubs at ends of house look lost

Driveway gets crowded & ugly!!

ATTRACTIVE OLD TREE

AIR CONDITION UNIT IS UNSIGHTLY

Arrival is very plain!

SHORT FRONT YARD—WALKWAY NEEDS MORE SEPARATION FROM STREET

NORTH

← S T R E E T →

EXISTING CONDITIONS

Project 4: Assigning Priorities and Diagramming Activity Zones

Objective: This project combines Steps 4 and 5 from the text. The objective of assigning priorities is to encourage you, the designer, to produce a culled list of things you want that are rated as to their importance. It forces you to decide what you want and how much. The second part of Project 4 is designed to help you understand how the landscape functions. Diagramming begins to show where different activities take place and how they relate to one another.

EXERCISE 1—THE PRIORITY LIST

Make up a list of the things you want in your landscape and assign them priorities as described in Chapter 5 as Step 4.

EXERCISE 2—DIAGRAMMING

Again use a piece of tracing paper over your base map or make a xeroxed copy of it. Blueprints of the base map can also be used.

First, diagram the three major *use zones* shown on page 34. They are identified as *public, private* and *service* zones. These three zones typically exist in any residential landscape. Very possibly they will overlap a bit, but that is expected. The zones should be drawn loosely as round-edged blobs.

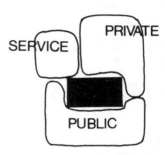

Now go a step further. Again using loose shapes, diagram all the major *activity areas* as shown on page 35. Be sure to make written notes within the areas to identify them. Label all the residence's interior rooms and exits, too, so the relationship of inside to outside is clear.

Project 5: Visualizations

Objective: To tap the creative imagination and encourage three-dimensional visualization.

Stretch your inherent imaginative powers by trying the four visualization exercises in Chapter 8. Now that you are on the verge of truly designing, your imagination has a big part to play. You need to "see" in three dimensions what your plan can only show in two.

Chapter 8 also stresses the importance and usefulness of little sketches or doodles as you get down to making design decisions. This is especially true of elevation sketches. An elevation is a view straight on of an object with emphasis on *height.*

Project 5 asks you to do an elevation sketch of the most important facade or side of your home as it exists and make some *changes* to it. Either add a view landscape feature or delete something that exists. Experiment.

There are two ways to do the exercise. Either sketch the facade freehand or use the slide technique described on page 51. If you took slides as suggested in Step 1 they should be ready for you to project onto a flat surface and draw off of. Photographs can be drawn directly on.

This exercise is an excellent way to test or try out design changes. In addition, it forces you to think in the all-important third dimension, height. Remember that it is a sketch we are after—not a fancy drawing—so please use something other than a typical pen or pencil. Magic markers, grease pencil, charcoal, laundry markers, or broad, thick pencils are better for the loose sketches.

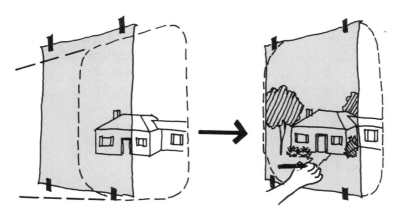

Project 6: The Design Scheme

Objective: To produce an overall landscape design scheme for the property.

Now you have the design pieces:

- An accurate base map
- An existing conditions map
- A prioritized list of your needs
- A diagram of the various activity areas
- An understanding (from your readings) of the basics of landscape design and an active imagination

Designing is the art of putting these pieces

together. Unlike most puzzles, this one has multiple solutions. In other words, there is no single correct answer but several acceptable design solutions. And remember that you, as the owner-designer-user, are the ultimate judge of what will work best for you and your property.

Having followed the five previous steps in the text's design process you should now be able to put some possible preliminary design alternatives down on paper. Again, these design schemes should be loose in nature and have plenty of written notes to yourself. Use the illustration as a guide.

Project 6 asks you to jump into designing

and produce a single overall landscape scheme that you will refine and finalize in the next two steps. Once again, make large xeroxed copies or better lay tracing paper sheets over the base map. Then draw two or three possible design alternatives. These preliminary design alternatives should be sketchy and loose, particularly at first, but fairly different from each other, too. Usually a designer will end up combining several good parts from the different alternatives into his completed overall scheme.

Before drawing your chosen solution, be sure to review and check your design against the list of common design problems in Chapter 9. Do not be discouraged. This is the hardest part! A top designer would produce a pile of discarded trace paper before reaching a good overall scheme.

Last, remember that it is the total property you are producing a scheme for. Do not spend all your efforts concentrating on just one part, and try not to be specific as to details. In the illustration the designer has only roughly located the desired features and named them by category—buffer, edging, and so on. It does not say brick edging or six-foot evergreen shrubs. The specifics of the landscape design come in the next step.

Project 7: The Finished Landscape Design Plan

Objective: Complete the landscape design.

Since you have followed the step-by-step process, creating the completed landscape design is fairly simple. All you have to do is take the overall scheme one final step. That scheme already gave you the basic layout of the final landscape design. All that is left is refining it and deciding on the individual details, such as dimensions, colors, materials, and so on. Chapter 10, Getting Down to Specifics, should help you make this transition.

Since the finished 17×22 landscape plan will be so much larger than the little illustration shown, it can—and should—show more detailed information. Also, if you draw the plan once again on graph paper, it will give rough dimensions since we have been using a scale of 1 inch = 10 feet. Because of this, the final landscape plan should be drawn with more care than the other project maps. Although there is still no need to be overly concerned with perfectly straight lines or fancy graphics, the final plan must be clear and tight compared to the purposefully loose maps drawn earlier.

Notes still need to be written on the plan. Only this time they should be in the form of specifications, not just comments. These written explanations and identifications will be helpful to you and to the contractors and nurserymen who may need to review the plan. So identify your changes. What was labeled as *buffer* and *edging* in the overall scheme now will become individual shrubs and 2×4 treated wooden edging or whatever. All similar items will need to be decided to really complete the design. Most likely, you have already made such decisions on many of the improvements. So much the better. Be as thorough as you can.

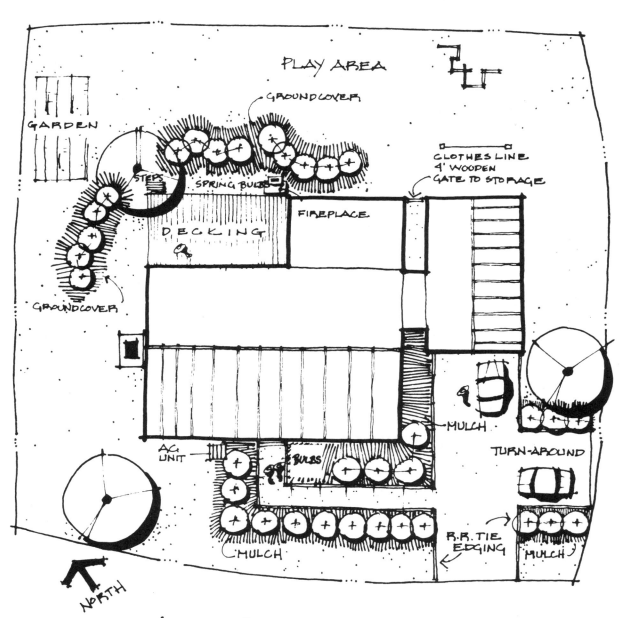

PLAY AREA

GROUNDCOVER

GARDEN

CLOTHES LINE
4' WOODEN
GATE TO STORAGE

STEPS

SPRING BULBS

FIREPLACE

D E C K I N G

GROUNDCOVER

MULCH

TURN-AROUND

AC
UNIT

BULBS

R.R. TIE
EDGING

MULCH

MULCH

NORTH

FINALIZED DESIGN

Project 8: The Planting Plan

Objective: To finalize a comprehensive planting plan, including chosen species names, numbers & sizes of plant materials to be bought, planting specifications and other pertinent information.

For many people a planting plan *is* the landscape design. Having followed the text's design process you know better. For a comprehensive landscape plan we first have to know *where* we need plant material and *what* characteristics the plants must have to meet our needs. Only then should we choose specific plant species.

The preliminary planting plan shown on page 103 takes you a long way towards creating a professional-quality planting plan. For many homeowners a similar plan will be enough. With as many characteristics noted as possible and the material accurately located, these people may choose to go to a nursery or landscape architect for help in the final decision making.

Those of you who want to do this on your own are already three quarters of the way there. For the horticulturists among you this is the fun part! Horticulture is a huge and fascinating field. Some homeowners will quickly make good, practical choices; others may prefer to spend months researching. How you wish to approach it is totally dependent on your own interest.

Searching out vegetation that "fits" means identifying trees and shrubs that have the characteristics you described and that will thrive in your property's natural conditions. Already understanding the site's conditions and the mystery of plant characteristics makes plant selection much less difficult.

Proceeding plant-by-plant is the simplest way. First, make a short list of possible candidates for each different plant material called for in the final plan. Then narrow each list down to two or three alternatives. It is usually relatively easy to find a few alternative species that are equally suitable. With these in hand the final selection can be safely based on personal preference as can the all-important factors of local availability and cost. Before you zero in on a prime candidate, try to see its alternative, too.

To prepare your initial short lists a little reading and looking is necessary. Numerous, excellent plant material reference books are available in libraries and book stores. The bibliography will start you out. Garden clubs, extension services and especially nursery catalogs are good resources, too. A decent nursery catalog will have available plants fully described and priced. Visiting local nurseries is an enjoyable way to scout out possible plants. The sales people can also answer questions for you. Last, just look. Be attentive to what other people have used successfully in the area. There is nothing like seeing a tree or shrub in the ground to grasp its potential for your own property.

Once you have selected each plant of the type called for, they must all be clearly located and labeled on the planting plan. How they are identified depends on the complexity of the design and the size of the drawing. With a fair-sized plan or a simple, straightforward design, the individual species can be labeled right on the drawing. Otherwise the plant material type should be numbered and a plant key provided.

Regardless of how the trees, shrubs and groundcovers are identified, additional specifications are normally given on the drawing or as part of the key. A final planting plan will need to address these items:

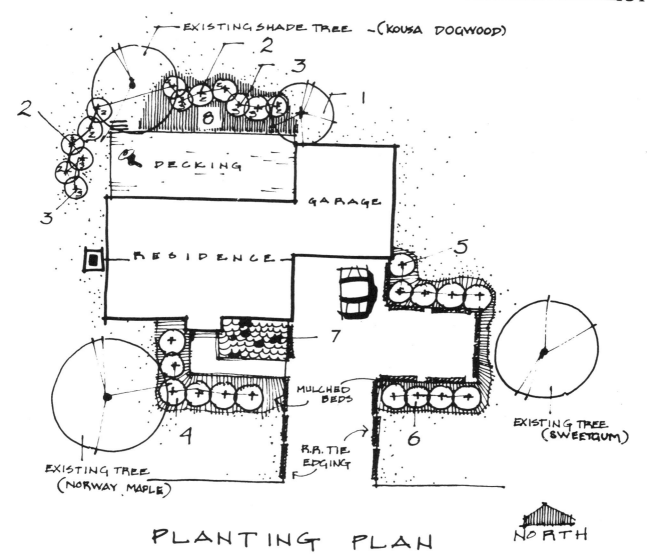

PLANTING PLAN

NORTH

EXISTING SHADE TREE ~(KOUSA DOGWOOD)

DECKING

GARAGE

RESIDENCE

MULCHED BEDS

R.R. TIE EDGING

EXISTING TREE (SWEETGUM)

EXISTING TREE (NORWAY MAPLE)

SAMPLE PLANT KEY

Key No.	Name	Quantity	Size	Specification	Notes
1	Washington Hawthorne (*Crataegus phanenopyrum*)	1	8'–10'	Balled & Burlapped	Specimen tree
2	Glossy Abelia (*Abelia grandiflora*)	8	2'–3'	B&B	
3	Azalea varieties Rhododendron varieties	5	18"–24" minimum	B&B or 10" pots	White & pink Flowering varieties
4	Mugo Pine (*Pinus mugo mugo*)	6	24"–30"	B&B	
5	Bridalwreath Spirea (*Spirea prunifolia*)	5	3'–4'	B&B	
6	Spreading Cotoneaster (*Cotoneaster divaricata*)	4	2'–3'	B&B	3' on center
7	Bigleaf Periwinkle (*Vinca major*)	7		2 year pots	12" on center, mixed bulbs, in clumps
8	Pachysandra (*Pachysandra terminalis*)	200		Flats	12" on center, planted in mulch

- Latin name as well as common English name.

- Number of each specie to be used.

- Size at planting, i.e., 2½–3′0″

- How they are to be received at the property—balled and burlapped, bare root, container, and so on.

- Plus any other pertinent information such as specimen tree, spacing between plants, and so on.

Reread Chapter 15 for more details. And remember to differentiate between existing and proposed vegetation. Existing trees and shrubs should have a dot ⊙ in the middle of the circle and proposed a cross ⊕ . The illustration shows a simple planting with an accompanying plant key.

With a final planting plan you now have a completed drawing that includes not only the selected plant material, but their specifications. Anyone looking at the plan will know *what, where,* and *how many* and be able to determine their size, condition at purchase, and any other necessary information.

It is truly a total, finished planting plan. With it the homeowner will be able to discuss estimates with contractors and nurserymen or purchase the plants and begin construction himself. Most importantly, he or she can now implement the plan with confidence!

Plant Material Lists

In the following lists of suitable plant material, the continental United States has been divided into nine climatic regions. However, within each region there is a wide range of rainfall, temperature, soil and other factors, so these lists should be used only as a basis for plant material selection.

If there is doubt about the hardiness of a particular tree or shrub in your area, additional information may be obtained from local nurseries, agricultural agents, botanic gardens and arboretums, and libraries.

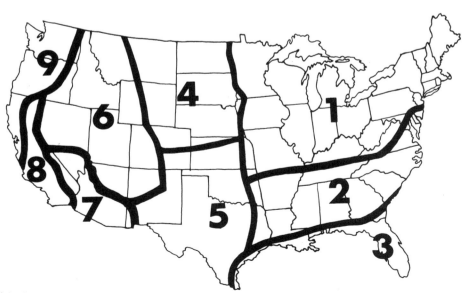

(v) after plant means varieties

REGION 1

Evergreen Trees

Eastern Arborvitae	*American Holly
Japanese Arborvitae	Lawson False Cypress
Deodar Cedar	*Southern Magnolia
Eastern Red Cedar	Austrian Pine 5
(Juniper)	Eastern White Pine
Cedar of Lebanon	Red Pine
Cryptomeria	Colorado Blue Spruce
White Fir	Norway Spruce
Canadian Hemlock	White Spruce

Deciduous Trees

European Mountain Ash	European Larch
Green Ash	Japanese Tree Lilac
White Ash	American Linden
Quaking Aspen	Littleleaf Linden
Bald Cypress	Black Locust
American Beech	London Plane Tree
European Beech	Cucumber Magnolia
Paper Birch	Saucer Magnolia
White Birch	Star Magnolia
Buckeye	Sweetbay Magnolia
Red Buckeye	Amur Maple
Northern Catalpa	Japanese Maple
Southern Catalpa	Norway Maple
Crabapple Malus	Red Maple
Species	Sugar Maple
Amur Cork Tree	Mimosa
Flowering Dogwood	Black Oak
Kousa Dogwood	Bur Oak
Fringetree	Chestnut Oak
Ginko	Northern Red Oak
Golden Rain Tree	Pin Oak
Eastern Hackberry	White Oak
Washington Hawthorn	Willow Oak
Bitternut Hickory	Russian Olive
Pignut Hickory	Bradford Pear
Shagbark Hickory	Thundercloud Plum
Thornless Honey Locust	Purpleleaf Plum
American Hornbeam	Eastern Redbud
European Hornbeam	Sassafras
Horse Chestnut	Serviceberry
Japanese Pagoda Tree	(Amelanchier)
Katsura	Silverbell
Kentucky Coffee Tree	Sweet Gum

*broadleaf evergreens

(Deciduous Trees cont'd)

Sycamore	Weeping Willow
Tamarack	Yellowwood
Tulip Poplar	Zelkova

Deciduous Shrubs

Abelia	Redvein Enkianthus
Carolina Allspice	Euonymous (v)
Barberry (v)	Forsythia
Beautybush	Honeysuckle
Buckthorn	Oakleaf Hydrangea
Cinquefoil Bush	Lilac
Cotoncaster (v)	Mockorange (v)
Dentzia	Privet (v)

Evergreen Shrubs

*Japanese Andromeda	Mugo Pine
*Mountain Andromeda	*Rhododendron (v)
*Boxwood	Dense Yew
*Euonymous (v)	Fire thorn (Pyracantha)
Heath (v)	Rose of Sharon
*Burford Holly	Rosa Rugosa
*Chinese Holly	Flowering Quince (v)
*Japanese Holly (v)	Spirea (v)
Juniper (v)	Viburnum (v)
*Cherry Laurel	Weigela
Mountain Laurel	English Yew
*Drooping Leucothoe	Japanese Yew (v)

Groundcovers

Ajuca (Bugleweed)	Ivy
Bearberry	Liriope
Crownvetch	Juniper (v)
Euonymous	Pachasandra
(v) wintercreeper	Sedum (Live-Forever)
Honeysuckle	Vinca (Periwinkle)

REGION 2

Evergreen Trees

Eastern Arborvitae	Deodar Cedar
Oriental Arborvitae	Eastern Red Cedar
*Camphor Tree	(Juniper)
Atlas Cedar	Cedar of Lebanon

(Region 2: Evergreen Trees cont'd)

Cryptomeria
Carolina Hemlock
*American Holly
*Chinese Holly
*English Holly
*Laurelcherry
*Southern Magnolia
*Live Oak

Eastern White Pine
Loblolly Pine
Longleaf Pine
Shortleaf Pine
Colorado Blue Spruce
Red Spruce
*Wax Myrtle

Deciduous Trees

White Ash
Bald Cypress
American Beech
European Beech
Cutleaf European
   Beech
Buckeye
Northern Catalpa
Southern Catalpa
Black Cherry
Chinaberry
   (Umbrella Tree)
Chinese Tallow Tree
Crape Myrtle
Dogwood
Kousa Dogwood
Crabapple
   (Malus Species)
Frankinia Tree
Fringe Tree
Ginko
Goldenrain Tree
Eastern Hackberry
Washington Hawthorn
Bitternut Hickory
Pignut Hickory
Shagbark Hickory
Thornless Honey Locust
American Hornbeam
Japanese Pagoda Tree
Katsura
Kentucky Coffee Tree
American Linden
Littleleaf Linden
London Plane Tree

Cucumber Magnolia
Saucer Magnolia
Star Magnolia
Sweetbay Magnolia
Japanese Maple
Norway Maple
Red Maple
Silver Maple
Mimosa
Paper Mulberry
Black Oak
Bur Oak
Chestnut Oak
Pin Oak
Scarlet Oak
Southern Red Oak
Water Oak
White Oak
Willow Oak
Bradford Pear
Pecan
Persimmon
Royal Paulownia
   (Empress Tree)
Eastern Redbud
Sassafras
Serviceberry
   (Amelanchier)
Silverbell
Stewartia
Sourgum
Sourwood
Sweet Gum
Tulip Poplar
Yellowwood

Palms

Cabbage Palmetto

Deciduous Shrubs

Glossy Abelia
Carolina Allspice
Beautybush
Buckthorn
Cinquefoil Bush
Cotoneaster (v)
Slender Dentzia
Redvein Enkianthus
Forsythia
Oakleaf Hydrangea

Lilac
Mockorange
Privet (v)
Rose of Sharon
Japanese Rose
Flowering Quince
Spirea (v)
Viburnum (v)
Weigela

Evergreen & Broadleaf Shrubs

*Japanese Andromeda
*Mountain Andromeda
*Japanese Andromeda
*Boxwood—
   Barberry (v)
*Camellia
*Cotoneaster (v)
Erica (Heath) (v)
*Euonymous (v)
*Fire thorn (Pyracantha)
*Holly (v)
*Honeysuckle (v)
Juniper (v)

*Cherry Laurel
*Drooping Leucothoe
*Mountain Laurel
*Mahonia (Holly Grape)
Mugo Pine
*Nandina
*Oleander (v)
*Osmanthus
*Photinia
*Rhododendron (v)
Spanish Broom
Yew (v)

Groundcovers

Ajuca (Bugleweed)
Bishop's Weed
   (Goutweed)
Crownvetch
Euonymous (v)
Ivy

Juniper (v)
Liriope
Pachasandra
Candy Paxistima
Sedum (Live-Forever)
Vinca (Periwinkle)

REGION 3

Evergreen Trees

*African Tuliptree
*Brazilian Pepper Tree
*Cajeput (Swamp Tea
   Tree)

*Citrus varieties—
   lemon, lime, orange,
   etc.
*Cocoplum

*broadleaf evergreens

(Region 3: Evergreen Trees cont'd)

*Fiddle Leaf Fig
*Lofty Fig
*Geiger Tree
*American Holly
*Chinese Holly
*Indian Rubber Tree
*Jacaranda
*Laurel Cherry
*Litchinut
*Southern Magnolia
*Sweetbay Magnolia
*Laurel Oak

*Live Oak
*Silk Oak
*Hong Kong Orchid Tree
*Oxhorn Bucida
*Pigeon Plum
Canary Island Pine
Norfolk Island Pine
Longleaf Pine
Slash Pine
*Silver Trumpet
*Wax Myrtle

Deciduous Trees

Bald Cypress
Bo Tree
Crape Myrtle
Cucumber Tree
Green Ebony
Benjamin Fig
Goldenrash Tree
Red Maple

Mimosa
Lebbeck Mimosa
Water Oak
Orchid Tree
Pecan
Eastern Redbud
Royal Poinciana
Sweetgum

Palms

Cabbage Palmetto
Coconut Palm
Cuban Royal Palm
Fishtail Palm
Florida Royal Palm
Lady Palm

Manilla Palm
Mediterranean Fan
  Palm
Washington Palm
Wind-Break Palm

Leafless Trees

Beefwood
Casuarina

Cunningham Beefwood
Scaly Bark Beefwood

Deciduous Shrubs

Butterfly Bush
Carolina Allspice
Cotoneaster (v)
Dentzia
Hibiscus

Bigleaf Hydrangea
Privet (v)
Quince (v)
Rose of Sharon
Spirea (v)

Broadleaf & Evergreen Shrubs

*Japanese Aucuba

*Azalea (v)

(Broadleaf & Evergreen Shrubs cont'd)

*Bottlebush
*Brunfelsia
*Camellia
*Carissa (Natal Plum)
*Cotoneaster (v)
*Croton
*Fatsia
*Gardenia
*Sea Grape
*Holly (v)
*Ixora (Jungle Geranium)

*Jasmine
*Myrtle (v)
*Nandina
*Oleander (v)
*Osmanthus (v)
*Photinia
*Pittsporum
*Poinsettia
*Princess Flower
  (Pleroma)

Groundcovers

Sprenger Asparagus
Artillery Fern
Sedum (live-forever)

Wandering Jew
Wedelia

REGION 4

Evergreen Trees

Eastern Arborvitae
Oriental Arborvitae
Eastern Red Cedar
  (Juniper)
Incense Cedar
White Fir
Douglas Fir

Canadian Hemlock
Rocky Mountain Juniper
Austrian Pine
Ponderosa Pine
Scotch Pine
Colorado Blue Spruce
White Spruce

Deciduous Trees

Black Ash
Green Ash
White Ash
Curleaf European Birch
Paper Birch
White Birch
Northern Catalpa
Crabapple (v)
Plains Cottonwood
Siberian Elm
Eastern Hackberry
Western Hackberry
  (Sugarberry)
Thornless Honey Locust

Katsura
Siberian Larch
American Linden
Littleleaf Linden
Amur Maple
Silver Maple
White Mulberry
Bur Oak
Northern Red Oak
Pin Oak
Scarlet Oak
Russian Olive
Yellowwood
Zelkova

---

*broadleaf

Deciduous Shrubs

Barberry (v)
Beautybush
Cinquefoil Bush
Daphne
Siberian Dogwood
Euonymus (v)
Pee Gee Hydrangea
Lilac (v)
Mockorange (v)

Siberian Pea Tree
Privet (v)
Rosa Rugosa (v)
Spirea (v)
Tamarisk (Tamarix)
Viburnum (American
    Cranberry Bush)
Weigela

Evergreen Shrubs

Juniper varieties
Bristlecone Pine
    (Hickory Pine)

Mugo Pine
Swiss Stone Pine
Japanese Yew (v)

Groundcovers

Ajuca (bugleweed)
Bearberry
Bishop's Weed
    (Goutweed)
Euonymus
    (Winter Creeper)

Juniper (v)
Ivy
Rock Jasmine
Sedum (Live-Forever)
Vinca Periwinkle

REGION 5

Evergreen Trees

Oriental Arborvitae
Atlas Cedar
Eastern Red Cedar
Cryptomeria
Arizona Cypress
Rocky Mountain Juniper

*Live Oak
Austrian Pine
Japanese Black Pine
Loblolly Pine
Ponderosa Pine
Colorado Blue Spruce

Deciduous Trees

Green Ash
Baldcypress
European Beech
Buckeye
Northern Catalpa
Southern Catalpa
Chinaberry
    (Umbrella Tree)
Crabapple (v) (Malus)

Desert Willow
Chinese Elm
Siberian Elm
Goldenrain Tree
Eastern Hackberry
Western Hackberry
    (Sugarberry)
Thornless Honey Locust
Huisache

(Region 5: Deciduous Trees cont'd)

Japanese Pagoda Tree
Katsura
Kentucky Coffee Tree
Mesquite
Mulberry (v)
Bur Oak
Chestnut Oak
Pin Oak
Post Oak
Spanish Oak
Texas Oak (Shumard)

Yellow Oak
Pecan
Chinese Pistache
Eastern Redbud
Texas Redbud
Retama
Sassafras
Silk Tree
Western Soapberry
Sycamore
Zelkova

Palms

Western Fan Palm

Deciduous Shrubs

Abelia
Barberry (v)
Bluebeard
Butterfly Bush
Carolina Allspice
Cotoneaster (v)
Siberian Dogwood
Euonymus (v)
Pee Gee Hydrangea

Mockorange (v)
Privet (v)
Flowering Quince (v)
Rose of Sharon
Smokebush
Spirea (v)
Tamarisk
Viburnum (v)

Groundcovers

Ajuca (Bugleweed)
Bishop's Weed
    (Goutweed)
Euonymus (v)

Ivy
Juniper (v)
Sedum (Live-Forever)
Vinca (Periwinkle)

Evergreen Shrubs

*Boxwood
*Cotoneaster (v)
*Elaegnus
*Euonymus (v)
*Chinese Holly
*Wilson Holly
*Yaupon Holly
*Holly Grape (Mahonia)

Juniper (v)
*Myrtle (v)
*Nandina
*Oleander
*Osmanthus
*Photinia
*Japanese Pittsporum
*Fire thorn (Pyracantha)

*broadleaf

REGION 6

Evergreen Trees

Giant Arborvitae
Oriental Arborvitae
Atlas Cedar
Eastern Red Cedar
Incense Cedar
Douglas Fir
White Fir
Rocky Mountain Juniper

*Common Olive
*Russian Olive
Austrian Pine
Ponderosa Pine
Rocky Mountain Yellow
  Pine
Black Hills Spruce
Colorado Blue Spruce

Deciduous Trees

Arizona Ash (Modesto
  Ash)
European Ash
Green Ash
European Beech
Buckeye
Northern Catalpa
Cherry Trees (v)
Amur Cork Tree
Plains Cottonwood
  (Poplar)
Crabapple (v) (Malus)
Chinese Elm
Siberian Elm
Ginko
Goldenrain Tree
Eastern Hackberry
Hawthorn (v)
Thornless Honey Locust
Horsechestnut

Red Horse Chestnut
Japanese Pagoda Tree
Katsura
Kentucky Coffee Tree
American Linden
Littleleaf Linden
Amur Maple
Bigleaf Maple
Norway Maple
Sugar Maple
Russian Mulberry
Bur Oak
Northern Red Oak
Pin Oak
White Oak
Russian Olive
Sweetgum
Thundercloud Plum
Golden Weeping Willow
Zelkova

Deciduous Shrubs

Barberry (v)
Beautybush
Cinquefoil
American Cranberry
  (Viburnum)
Daphne
Siberian Dogwood
Eleagnus (v)
Euonymous (v)

Pee Gee Hydrangea
Lilac (v)
Mockorange (v)
Siberian Pea Tree
Privet (v)
Rosa Rugosa
Showberry
Spirea (v)
Tamarisk (Tamarix)

Evergreen Shrubs

Juniper (v)
Bristlecone Pine
  (Hickory Pine)

Mugo Pine
Swiss Stone Pine

Groundcovers

Ajuca (Bugleweed)
Bearberry
Bishop's Weed
  (Goutweed)
Euonymous (v)

Juniper (v)
Pachasandra
Rock Jasmine
Rock Foils
Sedum (Live-Forever)

REGION 7

Evergreen Trees

*Carob
Atlas Cedar
Deodar Cedar
Eastern Red Cedar
Arizona Cypress
Haliam Cypress
*Eucalyptus (Gum) (v)
Douglas Fir
Joshua Tree

Rocky Mountain Juniper
*Common Olive
*Russian Olive
*Blue Palo Verde
Aleppo Pine
Austrian Pine
Canary Island Pine
*Desert Willow

Deciduous Trees

Bailey Acacia
Ailanthus
Arizona Ash (Modesto)
Green Ash
Chinaberry (Umbrella
  Tree)
Fremont Cottonwood
Chinese Elm
Siberian Elm
Ginko
Eastern Hackberry
Western Hackberry

Thornless Honey Locust
Huisache
Black Locust
California Plane Tree
Mesquite
White Mulberry
Pecan
Chinese Pistache
Bolleana Poplar
Silk Tree
Jerusalem Thorn

Palms

Canary Date Palm
Rock Palm

Washington Palm
Windmill Palm

*broadleaf

Deciduous Shrubs

Barberry (v)
Beautybush
Butterfly Bush
Cotoneaster (v)
Dentzia

Privet (v)
Ocotillo (Coach Whip)
Rose of Sharon
Tamarisk (Tamarix)

Evergreen Shrubs

Abelia
Foxtail Agave
Organ Pipe Cactus
Prickly Pear Cactus
Candle of the Lord
   (Yucca)
Century Plant
Cotoneaster (v)

Eleagnus (v)
Euonymous (v)
Holly (v)
Lilac
Privet (v)
Bristlecone Pine
   (Hickory Pine)

Groundcover

Bearberry
Bishop's Weed
   (Goutweed)
Hedgehog Cactus
Dwarf Coyote Bush

Dichondra
Euonymous (v)
Juniper (v)
Dwarf Rosemary
Sedum (Live-Forever)

REGION 8

Evergreen Trees

Oriental Arborvitae (v)
*Cajeput
*Camphor Tree
*Carob
Atlas Cedar
Deodar Cedar
Incense Cedar
Cedar of Lebanon
*Citrus Trees (v)
*Coral Tree
Cryptomeria
Arizona Cypress
Italian Cypress
*Eucalyptus
India Laurel Fig

*Jacaranda
*California Laurel
*Laurel Cherry
*Southern Magnolia
*Canyon Live Oak
*Coast Live Oak
*Holly Oak
*Live Oak
*Blue Palo Verde
Norfolk Island Pine
Aleppo Pine
Canary Island Pine
*Redwood
*Tanoak
Colorado Blue Spruce

*broadleaf

Deciduous Trees

Almond Tree
Arizona Ash (Modesto)
Chinaberry (Umbrella
   Tree)
Chinese Lantern Tree
Fremont Cottonwood
Crape Myrtle
Desert Willow
Chinese Elm
Siberian Elm
Empress Tree
   (Paulownia)
Ginko
Golden Rain Tree
Eastern Hackberry
Thornless Honey Locust
Jacaranda
Japanese Pagoda Tree
Black Locust
California Plane Tree

London Plane Tree
Magnolia (v)
Bigleaf Maple
Norway Maple
Red Maple
Mimosa
White Mulberry
Bur Oak
Northern Red Oak
Pin Oak
Willow Oak
Orchid Tree
Bradford Pear
Chinese Pistache
Poinciana
Silk Tree
Sour Gum
Sweet Gum
Tulip Poplar
Zelkova

Palms

Canary Date Palm
Mexican Fan Palm

Queen Palm
Washington Palm

Leafless Trees

Beefwood
Casuarina

Deciduous Shrubs

Barberry (v)
Beauty Bush
Broom (v)
Butterfly Bush
Chaste Tree
Cinquefoil
Cotoneaster (v)
Dentzia
Euonymous (v)
Fatsia
Hydrangea

Lilac (v)
Mockorange
Privet
Flowering Quince
Rose of Sharon
Rose Rugosa
Showberry
Spirea
Tamarisk (Tamarix)
Viburnum (v)

Evergreen Shrubs

*Barberry (v)
*Bottlebrush

*Boxwood
*Brunsfelsia

(Region 8: Evergreen Shrubs cont'd)

*Camellia
*Cotoneaster (v)
*Croton
  False Cypress (v)
*Euonymous (v)
*Fire thorn (Pyracantha)
*Gardenia
*Holly (v)
  Holly Grape (Mahonia)
*Jasmine (v)
  Juniper (v)
*Cherry Laurel
*Loquat (Japanese
  Plum)

*Myrtle (v)
*Nandina
*Natal Plum (v)
*Oleander (v)
*Osmanthus (v)
*Pineapple Guava
*Pittosporum
*Princess Flower
*Privet (v)
*Rice Paper Plant
*Tea Tree
*Viburnum
*Xylosma
  Yew (v)

Groundcover

Ajuca (Bugleweed)
Bearberry
Dichondra
Euonymous (v)
Juniper (v)

Ivy
Liriope
Pachasandra
Sedum (Live-Forever)
Vinca (Periwinkle)

REGION 9

Evergreen

Giant Arborvitae
Oriental Arborvitae
Atlas Cedar
Deodar Cedar
Incense Cedar
Cryptomeria
Lawson False Cypress
Douglas Fir
White Fir

*English Holly
*Madrone
*Southern Magnolia
  Austrian Pine
  Japanese Black Pine
  Ponderosa Pine
  Colorado Blue Spruce
  Norway Spruce

Deciduous Trees

European Mountain Ash
Green Ash
White Ash
European Beech
White Birch
Crabapple (v) (Malus)
Cottonwood

Amur Cork Tree
Flowering Dogwood
Pacific Dogwood
American Elm
Chinese Elm
English Elm
Scotch Elm

*broadleaf

(Deciduous Trees cont'd)

Siberian Elm
Ginko
Golden Chain Tree
Golden Rain Tree
Hawthorn (v)
Thornless Honey Locust
American Hornbeam
Horse Chestnut
Japanese Pagoda Tree
Japanese Tree Lilac
Kentucky Coffee Tree
American Linden
Littleleaf Linden
London Plane Tree
Magnolia (v)
Bigleaf Maple
Norway Maple
Red Maple

Sugar Maple
Mimosa
Northern Red Oak
Oregon White Oak
Pin Oak
Scarlet Oak
Willow Oak
White Oak
Bradford Pear
Serviceberry (v)
  (Anclanchier)
Silk Tree
Silverbell
Sweet Gum
Tulip Poplar
Yellowwood
Zelkova

Deciduous Shrubs

Barberry (v)
Beauty Bush
Bluebeard
Broom (v)
Butterfly Bush
Carolina Allspice
Cinquefoil
Cotoneaster (v)
Daphne
Dentzia
Redvein Enkianthus
Euonymous
Cornellian Dogwood
Siberian Dogwood
Forsythia

Hydrangea (v)
Lilac (v)
Mockorange
Siberian Pea Tree
Tree Peony
Privet (v)
Flowering Quince
Rosa Rugosa (v)
Rose of Sharon
Smokebush
Snowberry
Spirea (v)
Tamarisk (Tamarix)
Viburnum (v)
Weigela

Evergreen Shrubs

*Abelia
*Andromeda (v)
*Azalea
*Aucuba
*Barberry (v)
*Boxwood
*Cotoneaster (v)
*False Cypress
*Euonymous (v)
*Fire thorn (Pyracantha)
  Heath (v)

*Evergreen Huckleberry
  Juniper (v)
*Holly (v)
*Holly Grape (Mahonia)
*Mountain Laurel
*Leucothoe
*Myrtle
*Nandina
*Osmanthus
*Pachistima (Paxistima)
*Photinia

(Evergreen Shrubs cont'd)

Bristlecone Pine
   (Hickory Pine)
Mugo Pine
Swiss Stone Pine
*Privet (v)

*Rhododendron (v)
Skimmia
Viburnum (v)
Yew (v)

Groundcovers

Ajuca (Bugleweed)
Bearberry
Bishop's Weed
   (Goutweed)
Euonymous (v)
Ivy

Juniper (v)
Creeping Mahonia
Pachistima
Sedum (Live-Forever)
Sand Strawberry
Vinca (Periwinkle)

Bibliography

Brooks, John. *Room Outside.* New York: The Viking Press, 1969.

Church, Thomas D. *Gardens Are For People.* New York: Reinhold Publishing, 1955.

Conway School of Landscape Design. *The Home Landscape: A Design Manual.* Conway, Mass., 1975.

Eckbo, Garrett. *The Art of Home Landscaping.* New York: E. W. Dodge, 1950.

Faust, Ed L.R. *The New York Times Book of Home Landscaping.* New York: Alfred A. Knopf, 1964.

Ireys, Alice Recknagel. *How to Plan and Plant Your Own Property.* New York: William Morrow and Company, 1975.

Landscape Architecture Foundation. *Landscape Architecturale Construction.* Jot D. Carpenter, editor, McLean, Virginia, 1976.

Lynch, Kevin. *Site Planning.* Cambridge, Mass.: The M.I.T. Press, 1971.

Ortloff, H. Stuart and Harry B. Raymore. *The Book of Landscape Design.* New York: William Morrow and Company, 1975.

The Rouse Company. *Guidelines for Residential Planting.* Department of Planning and Design, Columbia, Maryland, 1970.

Simonds, John Ormsbee. *Landscape Architecture.* New York: McGraw-Hill Book Company, 1961.

Uttermann, Richard K. *Grade Easy: The Principles and Practices of Grading and Drainage.* American Society of Landscape Architects Foundation, McLean, Virginia.

Weber, Nelva M. *How to Plan Your Own Home Landscape.* Indianapolis: Bobbs-Merrill Company, 1976.

Helpful Books

Brooks, John. *Room Outside.* New York: The Viking Press, 1969.

Crockett, James Underwood. *Evergreens.* New York: Time-Life Books, 1972.

Crockett, James Underwood. *Flowering Shrubs.* New York: Time-Life Books, 1972.

Crockett, James Underwood. *Landscape Gardening.* New York: Time-Life Books, 1971.

Eckbo, Garrett. *The Art of Home Landscaping.* New York: F.W. Dodge Corp., 1956.

Moffat, Anne Simon and Marc Shiler. *Landscape Design That Saves Energy.* New York: William Morrow and Company, 1981.

Ortloff, H. Stuart and Harry B. Raymore. *The Book of Landscape Design.* New York: William Morrow and Company, 1975.

Wyman, Donald. *Shrubs and Vines for American Gardens.* New York: Macmillan, 1973.

Wyman, Donald. *Trees for American Gardens.* New York: Macmillan, 1965.

Sunset Books: *Decks*
Entryways and Front Gardens
Garden and Patio Building Book
Garden Pools, Fountains, and Waterfalls
Ideas for Landscaping
Lawns and Ground Covers
Walls, Walks, and Patio Floors

Reader's Digest. *Complete Do-It-Yourself Manual.* The Reader's Digest Association, Pleasantville, New York, 1973.

Weber, Nelva M. *How to Plan Your Own Home Landscape.* Indianapolis: Bobbs-Merrill Company, 1976.

Index